JFK ASSASSINATION: THE INTERVIEWS

JFK ASSASSINATION: THE INTERVIEWS

Volume 2

ALAN R. WARREN

VINCENT PALAMARA

Copyright

JFK Assassination: The Interviews
Written by Alan R. Warren
Published by House of Mystery

Cover design, formatting, layout, and editing by Evening Sky Publishing Services

Published in United States of America

ISBN (Paperback): 978-1-989980-22-4
ISBN (eBook): 978-1-989980-21-7

CONTENTS

Foreword

BY VINCENT PALAMARA

History's mysteries. It's what keeps events from the past alive for many. While there will always be a level of interest in past wars, tragedies, emperors, rulers, presidents, world events, and so forth, it is the intrigue of the unexplained or poorly "resolved" happenings from years past that capture the imagination and inquisitiveness to the highest degree. After all, relatively cut and dry landmarks from generations past like the U.S. Civil War and the founding of America have their place in the literature and the archives, of course. Still, nothing excites one more than putting on one's figurative detective cap to try their hand at attempting to answer history's mysteries.

Without question, the assassination of President John F. Kennedy on November 22, 1963, is *the* quintessential history mystery of them all. After all, you have a highly popular American president with movie star looks and charisma, who was the leader of the free world (triumph), brutally cut down (tragedy) allegedly by a sole assassin who adamantly denied the deed. What's more, the level of loose ends, unexplained details, unsatisfactory answers, and inadequate verdicts is enough to fill a mountain of books and articles.

Indeed, that is the case concerning the murder of JFK.

Oral histories are perhaps the best way for one to take in the often-complicated information from an author. In this regard, Alan Warren hits a literary home run here. Rather than consuming many books, one can come away from this book armed with enough factual data to enlighten and satisfy one's curiosity. That said, this work will undoubtedly lead a reader to want to check out each author's own books. At least, that is what one would hope.

They say, "controversy sells." Well, if that is the case (and, indeed, I believe it is), then one can begin to understand why President Kennedy's assassination has generated so many books, articles, and films. The interest is there from the public, as many millions of people still remember JFK in life. Many more have grown to know of him and his untimely demise via these literary and cinematic works of history.

In this volume, Alan Warren has compiled an eclectic mix of authors, some of whom generate their own brand of controversy. Indeed, best-selling author Judyth Baker is a lightning rod for debate within the research community, while best-selling author Roger Stone has made national and even international headlines with regard to his work for President Donald Trump (before that, Stone garnered some headlines about his work for Presidents George H.W. Bush, Ronald Reagan, and Richard Nixon, not to mention a controversial book about the Clintons). Author Barr McClellan, the father of President George W. Bush's press secretary, was part of a controversial 2003 episode of *Men Who Killed Kennedy* (as was Baker and Palamara) that had former Presidents Gerald Ford, Jimmy Carter, and the family of Lyndon Johnson protesting in earnest the views espoused on the program.

Authors Mark Shaw, Phil Nelson, Max Holland, Joan Mellen, Gayle Nix, John Koerner, Fred Litwin, John Barbour, and yours truly round out this interesting and eclectic collection. While everyone is not in total agreement about the facts of the case (to put it quite mildly), the various points of view are useful for challenging your ideas about the case. In some respects, it is good that authors who challenge the conspiracy notion of the assassination are included. They can strengthen or even weaken one's specific notions about this murder mystery. The give and take of counter-arguments can be a good thing.

History's mysteries. One would be hard-pressed to find a more important or fascinating one than the murder of JFK. We are all indebted to Alan Warren for adding to the literature of this case with this unique collection.

Vince Palamara

A proud contributor

Introduction

The JFK assassination interviews on the *House of Mystery Radio Show* have been one of the most contentious subjects that I have ever dealt with, both with the interviews and the listeners. After all, the JFK assassination is the grandfather of all conspiracies in America and arguably is where they all started. So, where do I begin investigating probably the most talked about murder case ever?

Many conspiracy theorists believe the assassination plot involved people or organizations in addition to Lee Harvey Oswald. Current theories claim a criminal conspiracy involving parties as varied as the FBI, the CIA, the U.S. military, Vice President Johnson, Cuban

Prime Minister Fidel Castro, the Russian KGB, the Mafia, or some combination of those entities. Public opinion polls consistently point out that most Americans believe there was a conspiracy to kill U.S. President John F. Kennedy. Gallup polls find that only 20–30 percent of the population believe Oswald acted alone. These polls also show there is no agreement on who else may have been involved. Former Los Angeles District Attorney Vincent Bugliosi calculated 42 groups, 82 assassins, and 214 people who have been accused in various Kennedy assassination conspiracy theories.

When I started researching this case in 2014, my first thought was to talk with Vincent Bugliosi; however, he was not speaking for several reasons: there had been so many attacks on his character after writing his books about JFK, but then, in 2015, less than a year after my first communication with him, he passed away. Unfortunately, this was going to be something I encountered a lot with this case. Almost everyone who had any personal involvement with Kennedy was now dead – meaning I would have to rely entirely on anything those individuals involved left behind after their death.

In the case of a significant event, such as a President's assassination, there is usually an investigation and subsequent official report. After JFK's assassination, all of the court documents and reports prepared by government agencies were combined into the Warren Report. The inquiry into President Kennedy's assassination, known unofficially as the "Warren Commission," was established on November 29, 1963, by newly elected President Lyndon B. Johnson. The Commission's 888-page final report was presented to Johnson on September 24, 1964, and was made public three days later. It concluded that Lee Harvey Oswald acted alone in killing John F. Kennedy and wounding Texas Governor John Connally and that Jack Ruby acted alone in killing Oswald.

The Commission's findings have proven controversial and have been both criticized and supported by later studies. According to published transcripts of President Johnson's phone conversations, some officials were opposed to forming the Commission. Several members took part only with great reluctance. One of their primary objections was that a Commission would ultimately create more controversy than consensus. Those fears ultimately proved valid.

The Warren Commission's records were submitted to the National Archives in 1964. However, an unpublished portion of those records was initially sealed for 75 years, till 2039, under the general National Archives policy. This policy applied to all federal investigations by the executive branch of government. The 75-year rule was intended to protect innocent parties who could be damaged by their relationship with those involved in the case. That said, the 75-year rule no longer exists. It was replaced by the Freedom of Information Act of 1966 and the JFK Records Act of 1992.

My interviewing of the JFK assassination experts started with some of the most popular books on the subject and lasted over six years. This book is an overview of the most compelling interviews from the *House of Mystery Radio Show* and it focuses on the highlights of what was gleaned from each guest.

All of these interviews, and more, are available to listen to on my website: https://www.alanrwarren.com/hom-jfk-rfk-mlk-interviews

The JFK Assassination

John Fitzgerald Kennedy, the 35th President of the United States, was shot to death on November 22, 1963, while riding in a motorcade in Dallas, Texas. While a popular President, John F. Kennedy was hated by some, a hostility completely related to his policies. Throughout my series of interviews with researchers of the assassination, Kennedy's critical issues during his short term as President were also the most common reasons thought to be why he was assassinated.

THE ASSASSINATION

Crowds of excited people lined the streets and waved to the Kennedys as they drove through the streets. Their car turned off Main Street at Dealey Plaza around 12:30 p.m. As it was passing the Texas School Book Depository, gunfire suddenly reverberated in the plaza. Bullets struck the President's neck and head, and he slumped over toward Mrs. Kennedy. Texas Governor, John Connally, was also shot in the back.

Their car sped off to Parkland Memorial Hospital, just a few minutes away, but little could be done for the President. A Catholic priest was summoned to administer last rites, and at 1:00 p.m., John F. Kennedy was pronounced dead. Though seriously wounded, Governor Connally recovered.

The President's body was brought to Love Field and placed on Air Force One. Before the plane took off, a grim-faced Lyndon B. Johnson stood in the tight, crowded compartment and took the oath of office, administered by U.S. District Court Judge Sarah Hughes. The brief ceremony took place at 2:38 p.m.

Less than an hour earlier, police had arrested Lee Harvey Oswald, a recently hired employee at the Texas School Book Depository, for the assassination of President Kennedy, and the fatal shooting of Patrolman J. D. Tippit.

On Sunday morning, November 24th, Oswald was scheduled to be transferred from police headquarters to the county jail. Viewers across America watched the live television coverage when suddenly a man aimed a pistol and fired toward Oswald at point-blank range. The assailant was identified as Jack Ruby, a local nightclub owner. Oswald died two hours later at Parkland Hospital.

CRITICAL ISSUES WHILE PRESIDENT

The Bay of Pigs Invasion[1]

On April 17, 1961, anti-Castro Cuban refugees attempted to establish a beachhead[2] in Cuba at the Bay of Pigs. The United States had grossly underestimated the Castro regime's widespread support, so the anticipated internal uprising never occurred. Castro's forces defeated the invaders within a few days. President Kennedy accepted sole responsibility for the debacle. Privately, however, he blamed the CIA and reportedly vowed to "splinter the agency into a thousand pieces."

The Cuban Missile Crisis[3]

Acting on his pledge to defend the Western Hemisphere if it was threatened by Soviet aggression, Kennedy faced the greatest crisis of his brief presidency in Cuba in October 1962. President Kennedy stated that the U.S. would intercept any Soviet vessel with arms and that the U.S. would retaliate if the Soviets attacked any nation in the Western Hemisphere. The U.S. Armed Forces were at combat readiness on "maximum alert." After a tense six days, Khrushchev announced his decision to dismantle and withdraw offensive weapons from Cuba in return for Kennedy's agreement not to invade Cuba and lift the blockade.

Vietnam War

The Vietnam conflict intensified, and U.S. involvement expanded steadily, although Kennedy refused to make any significant increases in support. By October 1963, the U.S. had 16,000 troops in South Vietnam.

Civil Rights in America

The Kennedy administration's most inspiring accomplishments were in the area of civil rights. However, the President did not live to see the acceptance of the comprehensive legislation he proposed. It was the most far-reaching since "Reconstruction."[4] JFK gave the Attorney General, Robert F. Kennedy, his consent for vigorous enforcement of civil rights laws to extend voting rights, end segregation, and fight racial discrimination.

The Mafia

The Kennedy administration made an effort to fight the insidious menace of organized crime. The President had first encountered the problem when he became a member of the Senate Select Committee on Labor Racketeering. Robert Kennedy was Chief Counsel of the committee, and later, as Attorney General, he became the President's surrogate in a campaign against the underworld.

Laos

Kennedy pursued a cautious approach in Laos, where communists had captured many of the northern provinces in 1961. In July 1962, the U.S. was able to get all parties in Laos to agree to a tripartite coalition government and withdrawal of all foreign troops.

The Arms Race

An escalating arms race and the harmful effects of radioactive contamination from nuclear tests deeply troubled the Kennedy administration. Despite an earlier promise by Khrushchev to join the U.S. in a "no-test policy," the Soviets resumed nuclear tests on August 30, 1961, and exploded 50 devices that Fall. Kennedy urged Khrushchev to join with the U.S. and Great Britain in an agreement banning atmospheric tests. When the Soviet Premier refused, Kennedy ordered the renewal of underground tests. In March 1962, after studying Soviet advances, Kennedy reluctantly resumed atmospheric tests with a series of blasts over Christmas Island in the Central Pacific.

INVESTIGATIONS AFTER THE DEATH OF KENNEDY

The Warren Commission

On November 29, 1963, President Lyndon B. Johnson appointed the President's Commission on the Assassination of President Kennedy. It came to be known as the Warren Commission after its Chairman, Earl Warren, Chief Justice of the United States. President Johnson directed the Commission to evaluate matters relating to the assassination and subsequent killing of the alleged assassin and report its findings and conclusions.

The House Select Committee on Assassinations

The U.S. House of Representatives established the House Select Committee on Assassinations in 1976 to reopen the JFK assassination investigation in light of allegations that previous inquiries had not received all federal agencies' full cooperation.

1. **BAY OF PIGS INVASION** – a failed landing operation on the southwestern coast of Cuba in 1961 by Cuban exiles who opposed Fidel Castro's Cuban Revolution. Covertly financed and directed by the U.S. government, the operation took place at the height of the Cold War. Its failure led to significant shifts in international relations between Cuba, the United States, and the Soviet Union. About 1,202 members of Brigade 2506 were captured, of whom nine died from asphyxiation during their transfer to Havana in an airtight truck container. In May 1961, Castro proposed to exchange the surviving brigade prisoners for 500 large farm tractors, later changed to 28,000,000 USD. On 8 September 1961, 14 Brigade prisoners were convicted of torture, murder, and other major crimes committed in Cuba before the invasion. Five were executed, and nine others were imprisoned for 30 years.
2. **BEACHHEAD** – a defended position on a beach taken from the enemy by landing forces, from which an attack can be launched.
3. **CUBAN MISSILE CRISIS** – a response to the failed Bay of Pigs Invasion of 1961 and the presence of American Jupiter ballistic missiles in Italy and Turkey. Soviet First Secretary Nikita Khrushchev agreed to Cuba's request to place nuclear missiles on the island to deter a future invasion. An agreement was reached during a secret meeting between Khrushchev and Cuban Prime Minister Fidel Castro in July 1962. The construction of several missile launch facilities started later that summer. Kennedy ordered a naval blockade on October 22 to prevent further missiles from reaching Cuba. The U.S. announced it would not permit offensive weapons to be delivered to Cuba and demanded the weapons already there be dismantled and returned to the Soviet Union. After several days of tense negotiations, an agreement was reached between Kennedy and Khrushchev. Publicly, the

Soviets would dismantle their offensive weapons in Cuba and return them to the Soviet Union.

4. **RECONSTRUCTION** - the years 1865 to 1877 following the American Civil War, when the Confederacy's southern states were controlled by the federal government and social legislation, including granting new rights to people of color.

Sins Of The Father

INTERVIEW WITH MARK SHAW

The place to start was with a book called, *The Poison Patriarch: How the Betrayals of Joseph P. Kennedy Caused the Assassination of JFK,* written by Mark Shaw, a lawyer turned author. The following is from the first of three interviews with Shaw in 2018. He wrote three very well researched books on the JFK assassination and was great at explaining his positions and displaying primary sources for them. Shaw is also a very nice man to converse with.

Q. How did you come to write this book, *The Poison Patriarch*?

A. In the 1980s, I practiced law in San Francisco with Melvin Belli. For those people who don't know, he was a bombastic, flamboyant lawyer, and in the 20th century, he represented some of the most famous people. With clients like the Rolling Stones, Tammy Fay Baker, and Muhammad Ali, he was in the middle of the action all the time. I got to know Mister Belli, and we became pretty good friends. So, when he died in 1996, I noticed that he had written two autobiographies. But the information about himself in the books conflicted.

He was known best as the "King of Torts." He was a great personal injury lawyer. He sued everybody and everything and got big damages amounts. So, when he died in 1996, I thought I would write some sort of biography on him? So, I did, in the mid-2000s.

While I was working on that book, I learned a great deal about Belli, and one of his most famous clients that people didn't know about was Jack Ruby, who shot Lee

Harvey Oswald. They also didn't know that Belli was very much affiliated with the underworld. His main client at the time, just before the Ruby case and the assassination, was Mickey Cohen.[1]

During this research, I interviewed a doctor friend of Belli's in San Diego, and the friend told me that Belli knew a woman named Dorothy Kilgallen.[2] She was a famous *New York Journal-American* reporter and author, who had a column spread to 200 newspapers throughout the country. So, we started talking about Belli and Kilgallen. He said at the end of the conversation, "It's interesting when Dorothy Kilgallen died, Belli said, 'They've killed Dorothy, now they'll go after Jack Ruby.'" That really made me stop and think about Belli and his representation of Ruby. It made me look back in time and see how it all might have fit in with the assassination of JFK, and the part Joseph Kennedy[3] might have played in the death of his son John.

Q. How did you tie Joe Kennedy into the assassination?

A. Well, the affiliation of Belli with the Mafia, and then his representation of Jack Ruby. As a former criminal defense lawyer, the defense of Ruby never made sense to me at all. You know this Psychomotor Epilepsy insanity defense that he came up with just seemed to make little sense to anyone except Belli.

So, I went back to the 1960 election to see what happened. That was just three years before JFK died. I wanted to see if I could focus on using primary sources and not speculation. What I found was that Joe Kennedy wanted to be President of the United States, and there was no question about that with everything I read.

Stepping up the ladder was the first thing, as he was appointed the Ambassador to Great Britain. He spent time over there, and unfortunately, before World War II, it was pretty well known that he cuddled up to Adolph Hitler. Joe got in trouble for that, and his reputation suffered a great deal because of it.

So, when he came back to the United States, he said, "Well, I'm not going to be President of the United States, because of my reputation being damaged, one of my sons will be." The first one, of course, was going to be his son Joe. Unfortunately, Joe died in the war. Well, who is next up? That's JFK. So, right away, as I learned, Joe put all of his money and power into making JFK the President of the United States. The first thing was to become a senator. Joe used all of his political power.

In the 1960 election, and you might remember, since this has been pretty well chronicled, they got into trouble with the election. They were up against Nixon, and it looked like everything went well after that terrible debate that Nixon went through. But they soon realized that unless they won Illinois and West Virginia, they would lose the election with the electoral votes.

One of the things that I tried to do in the book is to point out that Joe being involved in bootlegging and everything else in his past was really a lot of speculation. That said, Joe did have connections with the Mafia. One of those connections came through the Kennedy friend Frank Sinatra, who knew gangsters like Sam Giancana,[4] Carlos Marcello,[5] Trafficante,[6]and all of those guys. Joe went to Frank Sinatra and asked for some help in Illinois. Well, as you may remember, Illinois was as corrupt as any state has ever been in the world. That was because of Mayor Daley in Chicago, and Giancana was part of that with Daley. Joe Kennedy went to Sinatra and said look, “Could you do something for us so that we can win Illinois? And also, we’re going to need some help with the unions in West Virginia.” Sinatra did his job, and that is very well chronicled.

So, they win Illinois, and they win West Virginia, and they win the Presidential election. Well, there was a deal that was made, a deal with the devil. I have primary witnesses who were right there when Joe Kennedy made the deal – if the underworld characters, such as Giancana, Marcello, and those guys, helped them win those two states, Joe promised that when they got into the White House, they would leave those guys alone. They would not pursue those underworld characters.

Q. So, where did the trouble begin, and why?

A. Well, those underworld guys take people at their word. So, they are absolutely amazed and shocked when Joe Kennedy forced JFK to appoint Bobby Kennedy Attorney General. One of the most important parts of the book is that I have an eyewitness to that happening. John Seigenthaler was a presidential aide to Bobby. He became one of the founders of *USA Today* and a celebrated journalist. He was there that night when Bobby Kennedy said, "I do want to be Attorney General." JFK said, "I don't want to appoint him Attorney General." But Joe Kennedy said, "That is going to happen, and that is all there is to it." The next day Bobby Kennedy was appointed Attorney General.

Predictably, Bobby Kennedy, wanting to make a name for himself, had already gone after the mobsters in the McClellan Committee.[7] One of the first things he did, just three months into the administration, was to deport Carlos Marcello, the New Orleans Don and Giancana's best buddy, to Central America.

They deported him, and he was thrown into the jungle. It was just a terrible situation. He later returned to the United States. But that signaled to those underworld characters that Joe Kennedy was double-crossing them.

Through Bobby Kennedy, Joe went after James Hoffa, then Trafficante, then Marcello, and then they went after Giancana and all of those guys. One thing I'm telling you, you can't do is double-cross those kinds of people.

Q. So what happened next?

A. Well, as we get to the end of 1963, Carlos Marcello was about to be deported again, and he was facing a racketeering trial in New Orleans. His back is up against the wall. What's he going to do to get himself out of this situation? Marcello decided, "Look, I need to stop this. It can't go any further."

If he killed Bobby Kennedy, whom he hated, JFK and the government would have come after everybody, including him. But if he killed JFK, then Bobby Kennedy is powerless. And that's exactly what happened. They never went after those guys again until many years later, and Bobby wasn't involved. He finally resigned as Attorney General.

Now that theory has been confirmed by RFK Jr. He did it in an interview with Charley Rose where he basically said, "Yes, his father knew it was the Mafia," and pointed toward the guy who was in New Orleans.

So, taking that all the way around, what I am basically saying is that the decision Joe Kennedy made to double-cross the Mafia and appoint Bobby Kennedy Attorney General caused the domino effect until JFK died. In my opinion, and the evidence I produced, Joe Kennedy shot JFK. Certainly not literally, but figuratively he did because his actions caused the demise of JFK.

Listen to the full interview on my website at

https://www.alanrwarren.com/hom-podcast-episodes/episode/b3c5cb58/poison-patriarch-mark-shaw

---

1. **MICKEY COHEN** – a gangster based in Los Angeles during the mid-20th century. In Cleveland, Cohen met Lou Rothkopf, a member of Moe Dalitz's Outfit. Cohen later moved to New York, where he became an associate of labor racketeer Johnny Dio's brother, Tommy Dioguardi, and with Owney Madden. Finally, Cohen went to Chicago, where he ran a gambling operation for the Chicago Outfit, Al Capone's powerful criminal organization. *(https://en.wikipedia.org/wiki/Cohen_Gang)*
2. **DOROTHY MAE KILGALLEN** – an American journalist and television game show panelist. She started her career shortly before her 18th birthday as a reporter for the

Hearst Corporation's New York Evening Journal. In 1938, she began her newspaper column, *The Voice of Broadway,* which was eventually syndicated to more than 140 papers. In 1950, she became a regular panelist on the television game show *What's My Line* continuing in the role until her death. On November 8, 1965, Kilgallen was found dead in her Manhattan townhouse at 45 East 68th Street. Her death was determined to have been caused by a fatal combination of alcohol and barbiturates. She wrote front-page articles on the Sam Sheppard trial and later the John F. Kennedy assassination. *(https://thestickyfacts.com/dorothy-kilgallen-facts/, https://en.wikipedia.org/wiki/Dorothy_Kilgallen, https://www.bitchute.com/video/JEz57koe3O0o/)*

3. **JOSEPH KENNEDY** – a leading member of the Democratic Party and the Irish Catholic community. President Franklin D. Roosevelt appointed Kennedy to be the first Chairman of the U.S. Securities and Exchange Commission, which he led from 1934 to 1935. Kennedy later directed the Maritime Commission. He served as the U.S. Ambassador to the United Kingdom from 1938 until late 1940. With the outbreak of World War II in September 1939, Kennedy was pessimistic about Britain's ability to survive Nazi Germany's attacks. During the Battle of Britain in November 1940, Kennedy publicly suggested that "Democracy is finished in England. It may be here." Following this controversy, Kennedy resigned from his position. Joseph Kennedy was married to Rose Kennedy. During his later life, he was heavily involved in the political careers of his sons. Three of Kennedy's sons attained distinguished political positions: John F. Kennedy (1917–1963) served as a U.S. Senator from Massachusetts, and as President of the United States, Robert F. Kennedy (1925–1968) served as Attorney General and as a U.S. Senator from New York, and Ted Kennedy (1932–2009) also served as a U.S. Senator from Massachusetts. *(https://en.wikipedia.org/wiki/Joseph_P.*

_Kennedy,_Sr, https://www.whomarried.com/rose-kennedy-236540)

4. **SAMUEL MOONEY GIANCANA** – During the late 1930s, Giancana joined the Chicago Outfit. From the 1940s through the 1950s, he controlled the illegal gambling, illegal liquor distribution, and political rackets in Louisiana. In the early 1940s, Giancana was involved in Chicago's African American lottery payout system for the Outfit. In 1957, Giancana became the boss of the Chicago Outfit. *(https://en.wikipedia.org/wiki/Giancana)*
5. **CARLOS MARCELLO** – an American crime boss of the New Orleans crime family from 1947 until the late 1980s. Marcello had been selected as "The Godfather" of the New Orleans Mafia. *(https://mafia.wikia.org/wiki/Carlos_Marcello)*
6. **SANTO TRAFFICANTE JR.** – one of the most powerful Mafia bosses in the United States. He headed the Trafficante crime family and controlled organized criminal operations in Florida and Cuba, which had previously been consolidated from several rival gangs by his father, Santo Trafficante Sr. Trafficante was not believed to have total control over Miami, Miami Beach, Ft. Lauderdale, or Palm Beach. The east coast of Florida was a loosely knit conglomerate of New York family interests with links to Meyer Lansky, Bugsy Siegel, Angelo Bruno, Carlos Marcello, and Frank Ragano. Trafficante admitted his anti-Castro activities to the United States House Select Committee on Assassinations in 1978 and vehemently denied allegations that he had knowledge of a plot to assassinate President John F. Kennedy. Federal investigators brought racketeering and conspiracy charges against him in the Summer of 1986. *(https://en.wikipedia.org/wiki/Santo_Trafficante_Jr)*
7. **MCCLELLAN COMMITTEE** – The U.S. Senate established the Select Committee on Improper Activities in Labor and Management, popularly known as the McClellan Committee, after its chairman, Senator John

McClellan of Arkansas, on January 30, 1957. Committee testimony establishes clear links between organized labor and organized crime. It conducted 253 active investigations, served 8,000 subpoenas for witnesses and documents, held 270 days of hearings, took testimony from 1,526 witnesses (343 of whom invoked the Fifth Amendment), and compiled almost 150,000 pages of testimony. At the peak of its activity in 1958, 104 persons worked for the committee. *(https://www.michaelsmithnews.com/2013/02/the-enemy-within.html)*

Lyndon B. Johnson

INTERVIEW WITH BARR MCCLELLAN

One of the most popular theories behind the JFK assassination is that Vice President Lyndon B. Johnson was involved and responsible. We talked with several guests who wrote books on this theory, but I wanted only to use the most credible of them. The first guest we spoke to about this was lawyer Barr McClellan.

Barr McClellan studied at the University of Texas in Austin. As a student, McClellan was a strong supporter of John F. Kennedy. After qualifying as a lawyer, he worked for the administration of President Lyndon B. Johnson. Initially, he worked for the National Labor Relations Board, but in 1964 he became an attorney for the Federal Power

Commission. In 1966, McClellan joined the legal firm of Clark, Thomas, and Winters, based in Austin, Texas, and was closely associated with Lyndon B. Johnson and the Democratic Party. McClellan's work included advising on political strategy, campaign contributions, media issues, and labor disputes. In 1972, McClellan became a full partner in the legal firm, and at this stage, he became aware of the firm's illegal activities. John Cofer explained how the partners dealt with criminal activity: "In short, we helped plan crimes and keep the clients out of trouble." Soon afterward, he discovered that one of the partners, Edward Clark, had been involved in planning the assassination of John F. Kennedy.

McClellan eventually resigned from the firm after a dispute with Edward Clark. In 1977, he established his law firm. Some of McClellan's notable cases include litigation for exploding Ford Pintos, tobacco-caused expenses on the health care system, and cell phones' licensing and regulation. He also obtained a Supreme Court ruling to protect parklands from freeways.[1]

Q. One of the first things I heard about Johnson came from those tapes made of him while he was in the Whitehouse. A lot of what I heard truly surprised me, as I had never heard about that part of him. I mean, on one side, we hear that Johnson was the President that was giving human rights to minorities in the country, yet on these tapes, we heard him outright being racist, correct?

A. It really was. People will go back to the fog of history, and they'll turn to these tapes and say, "Oh, LBJ never admitted to killing the President." Well, he's not going to. But the bigger point was that the tapes didn't start until after Dallas and when he moved into the oval office. They're going to leave that out. But if you listen carefully, one thing about LBJ was he could compartmentalize better than anyone. For example, there's one tape where he's talking with some friends about getting money out of some counties back in Texas, and then he says, "We can't talk about that anymore because we're being recorded."

So, he knew what to say and what not to say.

Q. Was there anything at all about the assassination?

A. Well, it's just really strange. For example, he admitted that there was a conspiracy and that it was kind of a challenge. Yeah, there was a conspiracy, and my side pulled it off. See if you can crack it. It was so well covered up. You'll never find out, but there was a conspiracy. Again, the man could compartmentalize and talk against himself.

Q. How do you explain his background?

A. It has been well described by several historians: Robert A. Caro's *The Secrets of Lyndon Johnson's Archives* is probably one of the best ones on his early years before he was elected to the Senate in that stolen election back in 1948. He was always compelled to move forward. His father had gotten into bankruptcy, and his mother was so disappointed, she had pushed her son,

Lyndon, to do the best he could and not make any mistakes.

He was always able to manipulate all through his career a victory here, a victory there, even though it wasn't a victory. I mean, for example, he stole [the job] as Speaker for the small house. He manipulated the secretaries and that vote. He manipulated the vote to get elected in college and was later suspended. He spent a year doing some sort of public service.

He was elected to Congress with a minority of the vote. He only had 37 percent of the vote back in 1938. What happened was the congressman died all of a sudden, and they had to call a special election. It was set up to be high man wins, so he stole that one. Then 1948 comes along, and he steals that election. So, he had this overwhelming ambition. It's almost existential in the sense that it's 'whatever I want.' LBJ had no parameters of what was right and wrong.

Remember that he grew up in a time when six-shooters were carried around in Texas and when they had the Klu Klux Klan almost electing a Governor. You had lynchings going on and no respect for human life. So, this murderous trend, this murderous thinking, was part of what he grew up with, and he lived it out.

Q. We had a Professor John Koerner on earlier this month, and he described Johnson as having quite a few mental illnesses. He was a sociopath, paranoid, and he was bi-polar.

A. Yes, and yes, and yes. Let me explain. When Johnson came back from Washington, and couldn't stay in, and pulled out of the election in 1968, he went into a deep depression. Through the law firm, we hired a psychiatrist. This happened before I joined the law firm, or let me put it this way, before I was a partner. I found out about it later. But he had this psychiatrist who was trying something new and different against suicidal thoughts. He was trying to bring him around.

The last time I saw Johnson was when they dedicated LBJ Library in Austin to him. He was there talking to Ed Clark, one of the only people he trusted in my law firm. I walked over to visit with him for a minute, and you could see the easing that all the congratulations and praise he was being given was helping him. But he would quickly get back into it. (depression)

Two things we know for sure happened. One is after Johnson went to the inauguration of Nixon, he came back home and started smoking. Even his daughter said, "You're going to kill yourself," and he said, "It's my life." He had reached a breaking point. He was so depressed about everything else. The other thing that happened to affect his mental make-up that we know about, a lot we can talk about from observing him, but it's what he did that's important, and what he did was became a Christadelphian.

Now, this is a group that believes Jews are going to inherit the world, and if the world ends, it will be okay because the Jewish race, Jewish religion, and Jewish people will be there to take over. This kind of thinking is millennial-type thinking, where it's okay for the world to end, and this was part of his make-up at this late stage of his life. They were trying to cover it up that he became a Christadelphian in his last years. It was something that his uncle had been, and his father had been. It was kind of an offbeat religion. But in my mind, you can interpret that to being suicidal; it was that awful.

So, yes, he could be a sociopath. He could be unconcerned about legal standards in every which way. It comes down to what I said earlier, an existential belief of "what I want to do is right, and that's that. Don't get in my way." In my first book, *Blood, Money, & Power: How LBJ Killed JFK,* I identified the Penthouse records. These were recordings that the law firm kept in the penthouse of the building we were in. [Edward] Clark had put them behind a fence. It was strange. Usually, lawyers can see any kind of documents they want to. And we could have seen those, but we had to ask. And it was recorded. That was the only thing we worried too much about. If those records could be recovered, I think you'll find in there how the firm hired this psychiatrist and what he reported back. Of course, it's privileged because he was an employee of the lawyer, and the privilege would apply.

Q. When did you start to work for Clark and his law firm?

A. Clark hired me in 1965, a year and a half after the assassination. I got into the legal life in Austin. I had my own TV show, *The Law and You,* and had some pretty good cases. But with the law firm, it became obvious that once I saw, and was told, that Clark had planned the assassination, I couldn't continue. It was something that I didn't believe, but one of my partners said it. And what's said in a law firm is sacrosanct. It's what we know about what we are doing and did.

At one point there, they asked me to represent this guy named Oscar Wyatt, and there was no way I could do that. I had been representing some other clients on the opposite side. But they wanted me to do it, and they said anything that Leon Jaworski wants, we do. Of course, later, Jaworski would be the prosecutor, and he would also be involved in the Nixon case. He would be in charge of the Texas investigation into the assassination. So, he was a very key man. I said, "I can't do that," and they told me three times, "You got to do it. Whatever he wants, we do." I said, "I'm not going to do it."

So, my term there with the firm was over, and I left and set up my own firm. I went through a fight with the Clark firm, his big connection. I think this is true of most of the big law firms. They have a bank behind them like he was Chairman of the bank. If you have someone you don't like, unlike the Godfather, you don't have to kill them. You just call in their banknote, if they have one. So, they called the note, and I ended up in a big fight with them and the bank.

Ultimately the bank went into reorganization, which meant that I couldn't sue them anymore, and everything was thrown out a few years later. That's when I started investigating what I knew about the Clark firm and the assassination. This was in 1994. I started working with some other researchers and decided to redo some of the work the Warren Commission had done, just to see how bad it was.

We uncovered fingerprints from a fellow who had killed for Johnson back in 1950. We had his prints there at a local police office. They matched this fellow Wallace to a fingerprint that was recovered on the sixth floor of the schoolbook depository in Dallas. As far as I was concerned, this was really good evidence to go forward with what I knew had happened. And it was presented in due course, and it's in the book.

Q. Why do you think that evidence wasn't used?

A. Well, the print evidence is a specific and good example. They brought in a top-notch handwriting expert to prove that Oswald was there. At the last minute, one of the lawyers working with the Warren Commission said, "Hey, wait a minute. We have a whole lot more fingerprints that we've recovered, and we haven't identified them. Somebody is going to say there's a conspiracy."

So, they did this super rapid-fire analysis and ended up with two unidentified prints, a palm print, and a fingerprint, and we could go back over it and see the mistakes they made. The identification could be made. It matched to this fellow Mac Wallace, who had killed for Johnson, like I said, back in 1950. He did it again in 1961, but that's another part of the story.

Q. What about the Warren Commission and their report on the Crime scene?

A. The crime scene they analyzed and reanalyzed to the point that it's very difficult to get solid evidence. People are going to say, "I know there was a fourth bullet because there was a tree branch here, and it got nicked." How do they know that? How can they be so sure? This is the kind of speculation that the Warren Commission made to prove that there was only one shooter. They were blind to anything else because they were trying to say that this is not a 'Banana Republic' here in Washington.

Q. So there wasn't a single bullet?

A. They missed so much, or they pushed things so hard to make them fit – their theory on the single bullet is just about as impossible as you can get. The head snap, the headshot, when President Kennedy was hit in the head, he goes backward. They said it came from behind him. Well, he'd have to go forward if it hit him from behind. I mean, that's just the nature of bullets. They go forward. They don't bounce around and go back.

They also had, and this one probably answers the point about what you asked better than anything, the fact that Oswald was a marksman. I have a friend who is a former marine, and he said that if you're a marksman, you are one step above being fleshed out of the service because you can't shoot straight. It was this kind of thing. They just misconstrued everything. They could have never proven a case beyond a reasonable doubt, which they should have been able to do.

As I say in the sequel to my first book, *Verdict*, they didn't look at Johnson. And the first thing you look for in any criminal investigation is motive. Who had the biggest motive? Just to know it, and they didn't look at it. What they did, though, on the other hand, they did protect the new President.

They did a huge disservice to the one who suffered the most, and that was John Kennedy. If they had taken a look at who benefitted and who lost, it would have been an entirely different analysis, I believe.

Q. What was the purpose of them doing that? Was it just to resolve the case quickly to let American life go on? Or was it on purpose because they wanted to cover up for Johnson?

A. I think there's a lot of ways that you could look at it because there were so many people involved. I think what you just said is right. There were many in Washington who didn't want to face the fact that it might be a conspiracy and it might involve the government.

Everyone knew what a bad guy Johnson was. They had three Senate investigations going on. On the day of the assassination, they were supposed to kick off. The following Monday, they all got buried. They couldn't name the successor President. They couldn't even consider it. There were those that knew.

I'll give you a good example, Senator John Williams of Delaware was pressing hard and fought to the bitter end to keep the investigations going, but he was just one man. We had to protect the country. The rumor was that there might be a war breaking out, that Cuba and Russia were working together. There was this fear of nuclear war that impressed Chief Justice Warren to take the job. Johnson pushed him hard on that point. But to make it just one man, one gunner, one sniper, it was very, very important to keep it from spreading too, and it might turn out that Johnson would end up being one of the suspects.

Q. What were they trying to investigate Johnson for?

A. He had been working with Bobby Baker as his best buddy and had been his Secretary in the Senate. So, he had arranged everything like Senate hearings, getting extra clothes for a Senator who might have to stay overnight for a vote, women for whoever might need them at the Quorum Club, and the congressional hotel across the street from the capital. Bobby Baker was very important to him. But when Johnson became Vice President, that ended. Baker stayed there and did a few things that needed to be investigated, but there was this fear that whatever Bobby Baker had done earlier would land on Johnson's lap. One thing was that he had arranged to advertise on Johnson's TV station back in

Austin, the one my program was on. Anyway, they had arranged the advertising in a way that there was a kickback. There was a kickback for everything Johnson did. He took a commission on everything. That was one thing that was going to land on Johnson's lap, and they just couldn't have it.

Another one was this fellow Mac Wallace I mentioned, whose print we had identified as being on the sixth floor and having murdered a man in 1950 on behalf of Johnson. Johnson's sister was involved in a sex circle in Austin. This was right after Johnson had stolen the '48 election, and everybody in the state was getting ready to run against him. So, they couldn't let this scandal show up. Wallace goes in and just shoots this fellow, Kinser, four times, dead, in this little shop that he had. He gets off with a five-year suspended sentence, which is another part of the Banana Republic.

What I'm getting at is this fellow Wallace was involved with Billy Sol Estes, who was involved with Johnson since the '48 election. Johnson was moving up, and he needed money. Billy Sol Estes was really good at raising money and making it work. He raised a lot of money for Johnson. There was a 10 percent commission, which was the kickback given to Estes, from federal money, which would go back to Johnson. Over time, these crimes surfaced, and an investigator for the Department of Agriculture, [Henry Marshall] was going hard and strong after Estes, which meant that he would uncover Johnson.

Johnson had a meeting with Estes and Wallace in Washington on inauguration week. Johnson knew this investigation was coming to a head. So, he met with them, and this is well established, and told Wallace, "Go talk to him. Tell him we're going to give him a better job in Washington and to drop this case. If he won't do it, then he's got to go." I can quote that because the investigator, a Texas Ranger for the U.S. Marshall Service named Clint Peoples, recorded it.

So, Wallace took [Henry] Marshall out to Marshall's ranch, telling him to get out of it, and he refused, so they killed him. First of all, they hit him on the side of the head. Wallace could get pretty angry when he wanted to, and he knocked him out. Wallace thought he could now fake a suicide. He put a plastic bag over his head, turned on his pick-up, and ran the exhaust by him.

Well, that got started, but then they heard this car driving around in the neighborhood. Out at this ranch, you could hear it out in the distance. So, they thought, "we've got to move quicker." They laid him out on the seat of the pick-up and shot him five times in the stomach. He was probably unconscious when this happened. Five times. It was a bolt action rifle, so you had to bolt and re-bolt for every bullet you fired. And three of the five shots were fired. Somehow, Henry Marshall was able to shoot himself at least two times after he was dead.

Because of his control, Johnson was able, through Clark, to get the sheriff to say it was suicide. Before they could do anything else, they buried him. So, case closed, suicide. That's the way it looked for about a year. But then Estes, because these things fester, was indicted. He rushed to Johnson for help, but Johnson wouldn't even speak to him, even though Johnson had said, "This is okay to get this commission back to me, and if you ever get in trouble, then I'll help you." But that was just one lie after another.

That was brewing in the background for a Senate investigation in 1963 just before the assassination. It was this kind of thing that was hitting Johnson hard, threatening him. And the rumor was out that Kennedy was going to drop him. If he was dropped, he no longer had the immunity that goes with the Presidency. Or he thought he had,. That's an open legal question still. But Johnson thought he had the immunity of the Presidency because he was Vice President.

He was very afraid that he would be dropped, and all of this would land on him. He was facing either the White House, which was one heartbeat away, or the jailhouse. These kinds of things will motivate you to do things that aren't legal. But then again, when did Johnson worry about things that weren't legal? He had Texas covered back in Austin by his good buddy named Clark. How a grown man could get away with this is incredible, and yet he was able to do it.

Q. I also heard that not only was Johnson going to get dumped by JFK, but also when JFK was running for President in 1960, he wanted Stuart Symington to be his running mate for Vice President, not Johnson.

A. That was very much the case. Johnson had raised some questions about Kennedy's health, which was kind of a forbidden subject back in those days. Bobby Kennedy was particularly angry about this happening during the campaign for the Democratic nomination.

John Kennedy was considering two or three others, but I think any candidate was going to have a list to pick from. A lot of pressure just came up all of a sudden after John Kennedy was selected for the nomination for President, to turn to Lyndon Johnson, to be sure and get the southern vote. Johnson, because of his background, was racist. I'll just flat say it. He did nothing important to help African Americans, even while he was the Senate majority leader.

Perfect example, the NAACP was formed for one reason, to cut out the lynchings in the south, and they begged Lyndon Johnson when he was majority leader and even before, to support a bill to make it a federal crime, and he wouldn't do it. When you stop and think about something like that, it's just awful.

But it was important for Kennedy to add support from Johnson's states. Bobby Kennedy tried to get the decision reversed, but he couldn't. The tension between the two men, the President, and the Vice President, can be traced back to that point.

Of course, Bobby Kennedy was right there in the middle of it, and he was no friend of Johnson.

Q. Okay, so, Johnson was not going to be Vice President for Kennedy, and the different investigations that were going on about him, were they the primary reasons for Johnson to kill Kennedy?

A. No, I don't think they were the primary reasons at all. I think it had been brewing. You can trace it back to some evidence we have of planning for the assassination going back to Sam Rayburn's funeral (House Speaker of the House of Representatives), which was two years before the assassination.

Mac Wallace enlisted a Native American from Oklahoma, Roy Factor, who was at Sam Rayburn's funeral and later went to Factor's home to see if he could make a long shot. So, it was being planned two years before the assassination.

If you really wanted to trace it back, you would probably find it started back when

Henry Marshall, the agricultural agent, was killed by Mac Wallace. They had to be ready and have something in place in case it came to a head, and it did come to a head a year after the Marshall killing when they indicted Billy Sol Estes.

So, it wasn't just that Johnson found out he wasn't going to be on the ticket; it was an accumulative thing. Johnson was a sociopath and willing to do anything to become President.

Q. So, you think that the CIA was involved with the assassination as well?

A. Oh yes, going back to my first book, *Blood, Money & Power*, there were a lot of insiders who supported it and who could identify that the CIA was involved. In the history of the official investigations in Washington, the House special committee on the assassination concluded there was a conspiracy and that probably rogue agents of the CIA were involved. But they didn't know who they were.

This is another part of the story where it gets really interesting. Some of the names that came up, like "Trigger Jones" and a few others, are unusual. The "Smugglers Hole" is really where the history involves the CIA from what I've been told. Smugglers Hole is a little place down in a little town called Eagle's Pass. It was on the main road between Spain and Texas for many years, and then Mexico and Texas, of course. It was where the smugglers could go through and not pay anything. You know, free entry. They started using that when Cuba fell through this fellow named Robert Bibb. His father had been in Cuba when Teddy Roosevelt took his Roughriders down there, and he got a contract to export deer tractors to Cuba. They did it through the Smugglers Hole.

This guy Robert Bibb was a roommate of Lyndon Johnson during college, and they were the best of friends and stayed that way. Well, there were four men involved in this smuggling operation, and what they did was bring weapons and drugs into the country, and they got the Mafia involved in it. But they got caught and charged after Lyndon Johnson left office. Because his power to pardon was no longer there, they all got indicted. All of the rogue CIA agents were involved in the smuggling operation as well. When they were charged, they were all defended by Ed Clark.

This was all brought to my attention by a fellow named Jack Worthington, who came to see me. I didn't go out digging up this information; it just came in the door. Jack Worthington was told by his mother that John Kennedy was his father. Now, Jack looks a lot like John Kennedy. The case was presented to ABC and a couple of other media outlets in New York. ABC apparently stole some DNA somehow, and Ted Kennedy found out about it. He put a stop to them saying anything by threatening to sue them and telling them that he would own them.

When dropping the story, they were very unfair to Jack. Jack could tell me about both sides here because his mother was a Bibb.

So, this fits right into the Smugglers Hole and the rogue CIA agents.

So, you have this picture here that has emerged with Mac Wallace, who was being directed by Ed Clark, working with a couple of rogue CIA agents putting together a plan to assassinate the President. There was this guy named George de Mohrenschildt, who was a friend of Oswald. He also spent time with Bibb in Eagle's Pass. So, if you need a connection established from Clark to Oswald, now it's strong because this George de Mohrenschildt was the fellow that took Oswald under his wing. He was a former Russian, and he was also working in the oil fields, which is what brought him down to Eagle's Pass.

You had this fellow, Robert Bibb, who was account judge at the time, and his brother was the business manager of the family in Eagle's Pass. You can see how all the connections could be put together.

This planning was underway for at least two years before the assassination. But it was all still strictly off the cuff with people they knew could be trusted not to talk. That's who they could find through these many contacts out in the woods, so to speak, and bring together a team.

For example, this Roy Factor that he enlisted said, "Yeah, I'll shoot somebody." So, he told him to meet him in Dallas on December 22nd, and when he showed up, he told Factor, "We want you to shoot the President." Factor left. He wasn't going to have anything to do with it, but he didn't know about it until that day.

So, I think the story that you could put together, the history that you could put together is, they had the group who were committed, and you could leave Oswald in as what he said he was "a patsy," and you could leave Roy Factor there to be another patsy, but he bowed out and left.

Q. Did the CIA have their own reasons to kill Kennedy? Some of our guests have claimed that the CIA was running drugs in Laos and didn't want Kennedy to shut them down?

A. I don't think it was the drugs as much as it was the Bay of Pigs. The CIA had put together that effort to overthrow Castro, and back then, Robert Kennedy said they were not sending American airplanes in to support the freedom fighters in the Bay of Pigs. And, of course, the Cuban army was able to overwhelm them. So, the CIA blamed John Kennedy for that. It was a real grievance for some of them. In fact, the one I most closely involved, closely identified, corroborated is a fellow named David Morales. He was in charge of the CIA's, shall we say, the dark side of operations, including the Bay of Pigs operation. But the drugs were there, don't misunderstand me. That's how you could bring the Mafia into this. Because one of the four agents identified was involved with the bank in Eagle's Pass, the one that was a Mafia representative, and they were moving drugs. That was why they ended up indicted.

Q. Have you had any contact with anyone from the Kennedy family, and if so, what did they say about your book?

A. Yes, I did. When I put my book out, I started getting calls from the Kennedys. One of them was the historian for the Kennedy family. I got the card that Kennedy used when he was back in the navy, and I also have the gown that he was christened in. But the biggest contact on the Kennedy side was this lady Meg Azzoni, who had dated John Junior and had breakfast with Jackie. Meg said that she had mentioned Lyndon Johnson once, and there was dead silence. Jackie wasn't going to talk about him or let him be mentioned. Then Jackie resumed the conversation, not talking about Johnson at all.

She could tell me things from deep inside the Kennedy family. Like Jackie once told a fellow with the bank back when the assassination happened, that she almost lost her mind. I mean, you can't imagine how hard it was for that person who was sitting right there with her husband when his head exploded. She did all she could do to help him. This was a huge courage for Jackie to be able to do these things.

But Meg also had some deep insider knowledge of the Kennedy family because she was dating John Kennedy Junior. She was with him when they had one of the hearings at the House Select Committee, and John drafted a poem. This was a little Kennedy thing when they were together. They'd write poems to each other. I guess a literary foundation for the family or something. He called it the "Penaton Society." He was 16 or 17 when he wrote the poem, and he was trying to get America to say that it was a horrible assassination, that it was a conspiracy, and we need a parented nation to take steps to right the wrong. That's the first written evidence that came out of my contact with the Kennedys. She was also able to tell me that he took on a quest to find out who killed his father. When he had his magazine in the eighties, that was his whole ambition, and he was deciding to run for President. So, he could get deep inside and find out what happened. Of course, the tragedy was that he died in that plane crash up in Massachusetts near the Kennedy home.

Q. There are still a lot of documents about this case that haven't been released yet, and won't be for years, is that correct?

A. We need, and I'm going to make a formal complaint to law enforcement that there are some things you need to find now. One of them is I'd like to recover the Penthouse records that I mentioned earlier if they're still available. Billy Sol Estes has some records that need to be recovered. There's one record of a tape he made in a hotel in Austin, and Estes said he recorded it, where Johnson said, "Kill Kennedy." Bill Estes tried to record everything. He carried a briefcase around. A ranger who worked with Clint Peoples did the same thing. The story goes that he and Billy Sol Estes would go out in the woods to talk to each other, and both of them would record each other. There are supposed to be three copies of this tape, and we know of people who have touched on it or know something about it. I don't have subpoena power. I can't go in there, or sneak in, or something like that. But the FBI can or the police department in Dallas can. So, yes, we need to bring out this evidence. You got some big files with the CIA that need to come out.

Listen to the full interview on my website at

https://www.alanrwarren.com/hom-podcast-episodes/episode/770427b7/barr-mcclellen-bloodmoney-and-power-jfk-assassination-series

---

1. **BARR MCCLELLAN** - Spartacus Educational. https://spartacus-educational.com/JFKmcclellan.htm

J. Edgar Hoover

INTERVIEW WITH PHIL NELSON

This next guest also believed that Lyndon Johnson was involved. But he also thought that a strong motivator behind him was J. Edgar Hoover[1], the man in charge of the FBI at the time. This interview with author Phil Nelson was in 2014.

Q. So what exactly was it about Johnson that led you to believe he could have been behind the assassination?

A. Well, I read a lot of the earlier books written about Johnson that showed he had a very checkered past. He was not above criminal conduct to achieve election victories, and all kinds of campaign finance irregularities were going on. All of that was documented back then. There were magazines: *Life, Look,* and *McCall's,* all had articles written in the early sixties, some even back in the fifties, that indicated Lyndon Johnson had a history of criminal conduct.

When I was in high school, some stories came out about this newly elected Vice President that didn't make any sense. For instance, in mid-February 1961, a story indicated that there was an airplane crash on the LBJ Ranch down in Texas. The interesting part was that this happened on the previous Friday. So, for three days, there was no mention of it. And then suddenly, here it was broadcasted. He had only been Vice President for about six weeks at that point. But it took three days to announce it.

The stories about ownership kept changing after the crash. It was troubling. The two pilots were killed immediately in the crash, but Johnson wasn't hurt. Just odd stories like that. It turns out the reason they were killed was that Johnson had ordered them to land the plane in fog at his airstrip.

That had been built by taxpayer dollars, by the way, on his private ranch just because he was the Vice President. The reason he ordered them to land was so he could fly up to midland Texas, meet with Billy Sol Estes, and execute a criminal conspiracy to defraud the government of the United States of millions and millions of dollars. He and Estes could make that money and become rich. That's what we know.

Q. There's been a question about how Johnson got on the ticket with Kennedy as his Vice President. How did he end up getting on the ticket?

A. Through his association with his long-term friendship with J. Edgar Hoover, head of the FBI. And a man who, at the time, was respected throughout the country. That was really his ace in the hole. To have a friend who was as compromised as he was, who was as evil, and who was not constrained by ethics or laws because each of them was powerful narcissists. They were megalomaniacs, and this comes from not me, but from psychiatrists and psychologists I've quoted.

Basically, they have stated Johnson was a sociopath, narcissist, and megalomaniac, with bipolar disorder, paranoia, all of those things combined on both sides, psychiatric and psychological. When you combine them all, you've got a pretty powerful mix of attributes that can result in criminal conduct. What it means is that a person who has those tendencies has no guilt complex. In other words, they can do just about anything they want to do and not feel guilty about it.

Johnson moved in to be Hoover's neighbor back in 1941 or '42. He bought a house, one house down and across the street from J. Edgar hoover. I contend that he did that intending to become so close to Hoover that he could tap into him and have the resources of the head of the FBI at his beck and call. The only speculation in that whole thing that I just said was that my contention is he did that for that very purpose twenty years before. Whether he did or not is immaterial. The fact is that's what happened. By 1961 or '62, he had Hoover under his wing all along.

So, in 1960, when they went to the Los Angeles convention, the Democratic National Convention, Hoover was there along with a lot of other Johnson friends. By the way, Johnson had not campaigned for the presidency. A lot of people had assumed he had, but he had not. In fact, he resisted it. Up until about five days before that convention, he had not been a candidate to be President. The reason was that he wanted to minimize the risk of overexposure and minimize the risk of actually losing to this very popular Senator John F. Kennedy.

It was also his very fragile, inflated ego that he had to deal with. He knew that if he lost, either in the primary or the general election, it would shatter that ego. And it would be the end of his political career and the end of his political quest to become President.

He finally declared his candidacy five days before the opening date of that convention. He did so in a very awkward way, a very threatening way to Kennedy. He was actually intimidating Kennedy here in Los Angeles by spreading the word among the Democratic delegates at the convention that JFK had serious medical problems, so you better be careful about voting for him on that first ticket.

After Kennedy won on the first ballot, Johnson, and Sam Rayburn, the Speaker of the House, called him and told him they needed to meet immediately to discuss what would go on then. In the subsequent hours after Kennedy accepted the nomination, they met with him, and they threatened him. They used blackmail, and they used threats. The threats were that if you don't put Lyndon on as the Vice President, then he would become the biggest impediment to Kennedy's domestic agenda and that he would get no legislation through.

Kennedy had already extended the invitation to become the Vice President to Stuart Symington, a Senator from Missouri. This is all in Clark Clifford's memoirs. Clark Clifford had been a very respected aide and associate of Harry Truman and then John F. Kennedy. He was later recruited by Johnson to become part of his administration as well. But this is one of the most respected of all the men that served in these administrations. He said in his book that Stuart Symington had been the invitation to become the Vice President.

In the middle of the night, another meeting happened between Lyndon Johnson and Sam Rayburn. And with information from J. Edgar Hoover, which was presented to Kennedy as an ultimatum, by the next morning, JFK had rescinded the offer to Symington via Clark Clifford. Then, he offered it, under threat, to Lyndon Johnson.

At this point, you have to ask yourself, was Lyndon Johnson ever really seriously planning to run for President? As the top name on that ticket? And the answer, I think, is a resounding no. He never did that. He always wanted to be there as a second, as the Vice President, in an attempt to make himself the next person on the ticket. So that he would automatically become President in the event, John F. Kennedy died while in the office. And then he set out to make sure that that would happen.

That's the contention of my book and the reason I included "mastermind" in the title. Because only he, with all of the connections through the Federal bureaucracy, throughout the Texas state, and the Dallas political, police, and judicial machinery down there. He had connections throughout all of that. He was regarded throughout all of that as a very dangerous man. I've quoted people who had called him that at that time.

He suckered JFK into giving him the Vice Presidency, and basically, JFK signed his death warrant in acceding to Johnson's threats and blackmail.

Q. So, you think he had that in mind when he wanted to be Vice President?

A. Absolutely, I do. Absolutely, I do.

Q. Do you think that Kennedy had any inkling of it at all? I mean, later on during his administration.

A. That's a very good question. JFK never really properly assessed Johnson's willingness to commit criminal acts, especially murder. I don't think he realized just what a megalomaniac and sociopath he had there. However, I do believe that over time, he did.

As a matter of fact, it was evidenced through the records kept by JFK's secretary, Evelyn Lincoln. Her records indicated that the face-to-face time Johnson spent with Kennedy decreased every month throughout the first two and a half years they were in that administration together. Every year he spent less and less time. Every year Kennedy put him on an airplane and sent him off somewhere else – a funeral, or whatever, around the world. Just to try and keep him occupied and out of his hair.

But, in the meantime, I believe Johnson was working with his contacts through the back channels, so to speak. The people he knew very closely in the Pentagon and at the CIA and FBI, you know his buddy J. Edgar Hoover, and James Rowley, a very close associate of Hoover, who was put in charge of the Secret Service. He had contacts through these people and back in Texas.

In my second book, by the way, *LBJ from Mastermind to the Colossus,* the first chapter addresses a Texas Ranger, Clint Peoples, who pursued Johnson's criminal acts for thirty-some years. He was on to him, but he knew what he was up against, however. Because Johnson had made sure that all of his crimes were kept two to three layers insulated from himself, he would always have the deniability factor. You know plausible deniability going on. As a result, he was able to keep his associations with Billy Sol Estes, Bobby Baker, and others in his criminal contacts separated from himself. So, he was never really labeled on a legal basis with an association with Billy Sol Estes, or for that matter, Bobby Baker.

However, it was always there. In fact, it was in newspapers throughout the United States. Between March and September of 1962, you could probably look at a newspaper in the country, and there would be a story in there that tied Lyndon Johnson to Billy Sol Estes. Yet, the primary biographers, and the most famed biographers of LBJ, don't mention that at all. Hundreds of articles I'm talking about. Major articles that tie them together not only during this time but later when Billy Sol Estes went to trial. The courtroom was filled with photographers, cameramen, and reporters. It was a circus in October of 1962, and these biographers missed out completely.

Estes was credible, and that's not coming from Phil Nelson. That's coming from the U.S. Texas Ranger Clint Peoples, who later became a U.S. Marshall. It was him, and that whole chapter is about 40 pages of my book, that summarized his 35-yearlong pursuit of Lyndon Johnson. It's not something that you can just make up, but the problem was he was up against the juggernaut of the Johnson people.

And one of those people was a U.S. Attorney down in Texas, who put himself in a position of protecting the files that were presented to a 1962 Grand Jury. The files were put together by Ranger Peoples to try and reverse the finding of "suicide" that had been assigned to this fellow named Henry Marshall.

Henry Marshall was this U.S. Department of Agriculture. I guess you'd call him an "Extension Agent." In other words, he worked in Texas, and his job was to see that the rules were being followed in relation to, and I'm going to specifically talk about, cotton allotments. Back then, there was a huge surplus of cotton, and the government decided that they were going to have price supports. Congress voted in favor of all of these price supports so there would be subsidies for the cotton farmers. But the catch was they could not expand the ground or the acreage of where they were allowed to plant cotton.

Well, Estes figured out a way to get around some of that. They were building the interstate system through the southeast and southwest at that time. So, he went around to all the farmers who had land expropriated for the highways. When they lost land for the highway, they were able to reassign acreage through certain rules. If they could replace it with land nearby, then they could take that land and put their cotton allotment on this other land.

The long and short of it was that Estes figured out a way to have these farmers, who lost that cotton allotment, reassign that acreage to him if he bought it. So, he set up a plan with hundreds and thousands of these farmers to buy their land with the understanding that they didn't have to pay him a dime. He would then foreclose on their land, take it for himself, then put the acreage cotton allotment on it, and be able to harvest and plant all kinds of cotton.

Now I don't want to get too deep in the weeds on that one, but there are some complex transactions going on there that enabled the two of them, Estes, and Johnson, to defraud the government of millions of dollars. That's the important point that you got to understand. That's what it was all about. They were defrauding the government of millions of dollars through these schemes.

Well, here's Henry Marshall standing in the middle of that, and he was not going to allow it to happen. He was following the rules that he had been given to follow. He was trying to do his job. The result was that he was standing in the way. So finally, Johnson told his men, "He's got to go." That was the phrase he used, and they knew what it meant. He had to go permanently, forever gone. In other words, he had to be killed. From then on, whenever he ordered someone to be eliminated, it was cast in that wording, "He's got to go." So, they knew that, and they made sure it happened.

This was how he conducted his whole life, and Henry Marshall was just one. There were many people who were eliminated. In fact, there were at least half a dozen that were related to this one device. This thing that he had going on with Billy Sol Estes.

So, all these people were being killed, and they were being ruled as suicides or accidents. That just followed him around, and that's the situation that existed back in 1962. *Life Magazine* was reporting on it, and part of the report was that the Kennedy's were on to them. The Kennedy's were determined that he would not be on the 1964 ticket.

Q. What was the involvement, if any, in the RFK assassination?

A. Let's go back to March 15th of 1968 when the New Hampshire primary occurred, and Johnson barely squeaked by. Essentially, he lost to Eugene McCarthy, the peace candidate.

From that point on, he knew he was in big trouble. He knew that Bobby Kennedy wanted to join the race. He knew it for months, and he was worried about it. It was really a concern for him because he knew that if Bobby Kennedy ever became President, his sorry story and the whole mythical business of the Warren Report would be exposed for the lie that it was. He knew that Bobby Kennedy was out to get the truth.

Two days later, Bobby Kennedy officially entered the race. So, now we advance to two more weeks to March 31st. That's when Johnson came on television and announced to the world that he just decided that the job was too much for him and he had to resign.

Q. So, why would he give up so easily?

A. Well, one answer might be because he knew that something bad was going to happen to Robert Kennedy, and he wanted to be out of the picture. He wanted to have his name removed as a contender for the very office that Robert Kennedy had just announced he wanted to pursue.

It would have been bad form for him to stay there as President and continue running because then he would have a motive for the assassination. People would start pointing at him, as they had been doing for the JFK assassination, for the last three or four years.

Five days later, Martin Luther King was killed in Memphis. In my second book, I cover in detail why Johnson and J. Edgar Hoover's hands were all over that. In Chapter Six of my new book, I cover Robert F. Kennedy's assassination in Los Angeles just a few weeks later, on June 5th, and why all the same patterns existed in Dallas, Memphis, and here again, in Los Angeles. There can be no doubt at this point that the three major assassinations of the 1960s were all guided by Lyndon Johnson and J. Edgar Hoover.

Q. How was the relationship between Jackie and LBJ?

A. She had a superficial relationship with him. You could hear telephone conversations where she was sort of giddy when she talked to him because she knew what he was looking for. Yet, we've heard enough from other sources to indicate that it was just a front and that she suspected him all along. There's been a lot of reports in the last few years. Some from European sources, some Kennedy insiders, but none of the major Kennedy family members have come out with any comments related to Lyndon Johnson.

Robert F. Kennedy Jr. did speak in Dallas in January 2013 with his sister. They appeared with Charlie Rose of all people in Dallas. Although some interview clips were shown, the whole interview has never been shown that I know of. Yet they made an appearance there and had a lengthy interview. Whatever became of that, I don't know.

Enough has been said on the periphery and in other reports. Some of those were unsubstantiated, and some were saying that they came from Caroline. She held back because she didn't want her mother's personal affairs to become public.

There are all kinds of reasons the Kennedys have held back on laying it all out. So, I don't know anything about all of that, but I hope that someday someone will realize it's about time to get to the bottom of all this and make Jackie Kennedy's real feelings available. My understanding is that she had interviews with Arthur Schlesinger Jr., where she told him that she felt Lyndon Johnson was behind it. So, until those are released, I guess we'll never know.

Q. I guess there is still a hold on a lot of the files for a number of years, correct?

A. Yes, and in 1964, that was the first thing that caused me to start questioning what in the world was going on. Because here they were, on the one hand, led by Johnson, of course, saying it was a lone nut. Just some "screwball, misinformed, and maladjusted commie guy" that decided he was going to murder the U.S. President, and up and did it.

That was the story. But as implausible as it was then, it really became ridiculous later when the very same people in the government said, "Oh, we're going to have to put this all this on hold and bury it for 75 years." Everything was going to be buried for 75 years initially. That didn't change until Oliver Stone's movie, *JFK*, came out in 1991.

In 1992, Congress reacted and voted unanimously that all of those restrictions are now going to be replaced with the JFK Records Retention Act. This Act stated that all government agencies had to release all information they had regarding the assassinations of JFK, Martin Luther King, and Robert Kennedy. And they had to be released as quickly as possible.

I don't remember exactly what the deadlines were, but after that, certain records started being released, and it opened up new areas for research. That was the result of the passing of the legislation. The problem with the final date set of 2017, originally 2039, I believe, is how much left will be meaningful. It's anybody's guess. It never made sense to anybody to have all of the data and all the records frozen and put aside and made secret for 75 years, which is what it originally was.

Q. Do you believe that Lee Harvey Oswald was involved in the assassination?

A. No, I don't. He might have been in the periphery but unbeknownst to him, that he was going to be the patsy. When it came down, he quickly realized that he was the patsy. He even said it on national television as he was being arrested.

But he was clearly not on the sixth floor. He was down on the main floor of the Texas Schoolbook Depository and had been out on the front portico watching the procession. As soon as it went by, he went back inside, and he was found there just a minute or two later by the police. One policeman, in particular, came running in and encountered him. He was drinking a coke, and he had not been out of breath and had no signs that he had rushed down from his sniper's purse, so to speak.

Regardless, people still try to rationalize it. They rationalize this. They rationalize that. But nothing made sense when you really put it together. Yet, there are many people out there who still believe it, by God, because that's what the government said.

Q. So, do you have any idea who actually did the shooting?

A. That's something I have not really explored much because to me, it doesn't matter as much as who was behind it. The actual shooters could have been anybody.

There have been a lot of people who have since confessed, and they want you to believe they were the shooters. It might have been James Files. I just don't know. And I'd rather not comment on that because that's a real rabbit hole.

Listen to the full interview on my website at

> https://www.alanrwarren.com/
> hom-podcast-episodes/
> episode/b8262958/phil-
> nelson-lbj-mastermind-jfk-
> assassination-series

---

1. **JOHN EDGAR HOOVER** – the first Director of the Federal Bureau of Investigation of the United States. Hoover personally directed the FBI investigation of the assassination of President John F. Kennedy. In 1964, just days before Hoover testified in the earliest stages of the Warren Commission hearings, President Lyndon B. Johnson waived the then-mandatory U.S. Government Service Retirement Age of 70, allowing Hoover to remain the FBI Director "for an indefinite period of time." The House Select Committee on Assassinations issued a report in 1979 critical of the performance by the FBI, the Warren Commission, and other agencies. The report criticized the FBI's Hoover's reluctance to investigate thoroughly the possibility of a conspiracy to assassinate the President. *(https://en.wikipedia.org/wiki/Edgar_Hoover)*

The Mafia

INTERVIEW WITH ROGER STONE

When you call yourself an "Alternative Historian," as Roger Stone does, we had to approach him cautiously. I included this interview because Stone was the primary man behind most conspiracy theories written about throughout the years. Most of his claims have no hard evidence behind them. Lack of evidence is a primary issue for this investigation as it's primarily derived from the author's feelings towards certain people.

Following this chapter, I have included the interview with Joan Mellen, who presents evidence disputing what Stone has claimed. In fact, throughout the rest of this book, you will find all of Stone's claims seem to have just been driven by his personal feelings and no real evidence.

Q. Let's start with what led you to think that LBJ could have done something such as kill Kennedy?

A. I think Lyndon Johnson had the motive, means, and opportunity to kill John F. Kennedy. By 1963, Johnson was under siege in two Federal investigations that threatened to expose him and send him to prison. He was at the epicenter of the Bobby Baker[1] investigation. In fact, the Senate investigation into the Baker affair, where Baker has been splitting bribes with Johnson, opened in the Senate on November 22, 1963.

Johnson was on the phone throughout that fateful day with his aides in Washington to see whether his name had surfaced in those open hearings where Senator Williams of Delaware had vowed to expose LBJ. Then officially, Johnson knew that the Justice

Department, under Robert Kennedy, had leaked to *Time Magazine* details of Johnson's involvement with Billy Sol Estes, a flamboyant Texas wheeler-dealer, with who Johnson was sharing other federal kickbacks.

Johnson was not just facing political ruin and being dumped from the 1964 ticket. The memoir of John F. Kennedy's trusted secretary, Evelyn Lincoln, stated that JFK confided in her that Johnson would be dumped from the 1964 ticket on the day before he left for Dallas.

On November 24th, Drew Pearson, the most powerful syndicated columnist of his day, whose column ran in over 700 newspapers, had already written a story tying LBJ to a $100,000 bribe he took to deliver the TFX defense contract to General Dynamics in Fort Worth, Texas. LBJ's ticket to the penitentiary. It was over, and he knew it.

Q. It's been said, too, that Kennedy never wanted LBJ on the original ticket as well?

A. That's true. He blackmailed his way onto the ticket. LBJ ordered the break-in into Kennedy's doctor's office to secure proof from his medical records that he had Addison's disease. As an LBJ agent, John Connally, Texas Governor, at a press conference at the Democratic Convention, attacked Kennedy for being too sick to be President because of his Addison. That's the kind of tactics Johnson used.

That was what began the deep animosity between Robert Kennedy and Johnson. Robert Kennedy stuck his finger in Johnson's face once he's won and said, "You and your people ran a dirty campaign, and you are going to pay!"

Q. So, what did Johnson use to blackmail Kennedy?

A. Johnson and Senate House Speaker Sam Rayburn went to Kennedy's hotel room late at night, the night before the Vice-Presidential nomination. LBJ shows Kennedy photos of himself naked in bed, shall we say, with various young ladies. The photos were courtesy of J. Edgar Hoover, who had kept quite a dossier on Jack Kennedy's sexual relations with an East German spy, with different prostitutes, and with a Nazi spy. All of this is, of course, in Hoover's secret files.

John Kennedy actually offered the vice presidency to Stuart Symington, and he had to withdraw the offer from Symington to give it to Johnson. Now that probably elected him as President. LBJ burned over 60,000 Nixon ballets in Texas, so Nixon won the election, but Johnson stole it for his running mate Kennedy.

Q. I have heard that Johnson had done illegal things in previous elections as well. Is that true?

A. Well, he stole his first election in 1948, and then he ordered the murder of a deputy sheriff who threatened to go to the feds and tell them everything. That was probably Johnson's first known public murder, but he would go on to order the murders of other men. Murders to cover up voter fraud, murders to cover up corruption.

I believe he ordered the murder of his sister because she was running her mouth about certain things she knew. He certainly ordered the murder of a man named John Douglas Kinser, who was blackmailing Johnson with the information he had obtained from Johnson's sister.

Kinser was murdered in broad daylight by a man named Malcolm Wallace. Wallace was in a federal patriot's position at the Agriculture Department, where he was a personal hitman for Lyndon Johnson. He murdered Kinser in cold blood, and he was apprehended. When apprehended, he said to the police officer, "Officer, you can't arrest me. I work for Senator Johnson."

He went on trial, and Lyndon Johnson's cronies bailed him out. Lyndon Johnson's personal attorney John Cofer defended Wallace at trial. Wallace was convicted of first-degree murder, but the Judge, one of Johnson's cronies, gave him a five-year suspended sentence.

Malcolm Wallace was immediately hired by D. H. Byrd to work for a defense contractor. Malcolm Wallace's fingerprint was found in the sniper's nest on the sixth floor of the Schoolbook Depository building. The building was owned by D.H. Byrd. Many witnesses saw Johnson's hitman Wallace, in the window of the sixth floor of the Texas Schoolbook Depository. Two witnesses saw Wallace flee the building after Kennedy was shot. There is fingerprint evidence and eyewitness evidence tying a Johnson hitman to at least one of the shooters.

I believe there was a shooter on the grassy knoll. I believe there was a shooter in the sewer grate and maybe another shooter in the Dal-Tex building.

President John F. Kennedy was killed in a crossfire with bullets coming from both his front and rear.

Q. Wouldn't the wounds on Kennedy show us this?

A. The Government went to great extents to try and cover this up. But the eyewitnesses at Parkland Hospital in Dallas, 13 of them, saw a gaping exit wound in the back of Kennedy's head. This is indisputable. By the time Kennedy's body got to Bethesda Medical Center, this wound had disappeared.

Q. How did Wallace die?

A. He died in a suspicious car crash in which someone had stuffed a potato into the exhaust of his pick-up truck. The cab filled with fumes, and he would ultimately drive off the road in a crash and was killed.

Lyndon Johnson had a cousin who was a dead ringer for him and sounded like him too. Johnson often used his cousin as a decoy in those instances when the Vice President needed to be seen and not heard. Shortly after becoming President, Johnson was displeased to pick up an issue of *Variety* and notice an article that stated his cousin looked so much like LBJ that he was hired by a television series for a walk-on role for the President of the United States.

Two weeks later, Johnson's cousin was brutally murdered with a shotgun to the face.

Q. Why would that be significant?

A. Why is it significant? Because we know that Johnson was seen in Fort Worth on the evening of November 21st, but he was not heard in Fort Worth. He was merely 'seen' entering his hotel.

When in fact now, there's a huge body of evidence showing that Johnson arrived in Dallas after midnight, for a secret sit down with H.L. Hunt, his righthand man Ed Clarke, Clint Murchison, D.H. Byrd, and others who were coordinating the final minutes of the life of John F. Kennedy.

Q. Now, I've heard that J. Edgar Hoover was at the meeting as well. Is that true?

A. Hoover was also at this party. The Murchison chauffeur said that he drove Hoover to a grass airstrip where he was picked up by a government plane at 3 a.m. Which meant that he could have certainly been back at his desk in Washington, as the records show was the following morning.

Q. So you believe Hoover was definitely involved then?

A. Hoover's main role was not in the plot.

In the plot, Johnson provided at least one of the shooters, Malcolm Wallace. The Central Intelligence Agency provided the patsy, that's Oswald. The Dallas Police Department, under the control of Lyndon Johnson, controlled the early investigation. The District Attorney, a Johnson man, controlled the early investigation.

There's no federal jurisdiction in a murder trial. So, the FBI's role came after the murder, when they were the agents for the Warren Commission cover-up. Let me remind you that Hoover did his own investigation and, within seven days, declared Oswald the killer and said he acted alone.

The Warren Commission now became superfluous. They either had to disagree with the published report by Hoover, or they had to go along with it. Well, they obviously went along with it.

In order to do so, Arlen Spector had to invent the single-bullet theory. He had to make one bullet disappear. Too many bullets, too many shooters.

Q. Why do you think they selected the people they did to be on the Warren Commission?

A. The Warren Commission was a commission of people that the Kennedys hated. It was Johnson's way of saying to Bobby, and the entire Kennedy clan, that he despised them.

Allen Dulles was fired by Kennedy, and he openly blamed Kennedy for the failure at the Bay of Pigs. The agency took no responsibility. Kennedy, they said, was a traitor. Kennedy was a drug addict. Allen Dulles was spreading the word that JFK was, in fact, addicted to crystal meth, which he was. Kennedy was injecting methamphetamines drugs by Dr. Max Jacobson, also known as Dr. Feelgood.

LBJ, the FBI, and the CIA were all well aware that John F. Kennedy was high almost all of the time, which explains his voracious sexual appetite despite the fact that he had a very bad back and was almost constantly in pain.

Doctor Max Jacobson's patients include Frank Sinatra, Marilyn Monroe, Nelson Rockefeller, Spiro Agnew, Joe DiMaggio, Leonard Bernstein, Halston, Roy Cohen, all the beautiful people of that entire period.

Q. What more can you tell us about Johnson?

A. I make a case that he ordered the false flag bombing of the USS Liberty by the Israelis. The murder of 36 U.S. servicemen that he intended to use as a false pretext for war with Egypt. Johnson was someone whose corruption was of biblical proportions. I show that he stole at least 1 billion dollars in gold from the Federal Government and that his daughters later unloaded this gold on the international market for as much as 6 billion.

Q. Who else was involved in the plot to kill Kennedy with Johnson?

A. Johnson had a unique relationship with everyone else who was involved in the plot. I think the plot involved the CIA, organized crime, and big Texas oil.

Lyndon Johnson was the paymaster for the CIA. Without money, the CIA could not fund their ops. Lyndon Johnson at on the aerospace subcommittee of the Appropriations Committee where the secret black box budgets of the CIA were buried. Johnson was the guy giving them more and more money throughout the fifties.

The Senate Committee watches if the CIA acts legally or not. Then, it was chaired by Senator Harry F. Byrd, Johnson's closest ally. So, Johnson had a unique relationship with the CIA.

The CIA's motives in the murder against Kennedy were clear. They blamed him for the Bay of Pigs. More precisely, they knew that Khrushchev had snookered Kennedy in the Cuban Missile Crisis. Russian missiles were never removed from the Soviet Union. They were headed for Cuba. Kennedy's deal with Khrushchev called for no on-sight inspections.

But the Kennedy brothers cut a secret deal to remove our missiles from Italy and Turkey. That was kept from the American people for forty years because it was classified. The Kennedy brothers showed weakness. They backed down.

Organized crime gave one million to elect Kennedy. They twisted arms for him in Chicago and the West Virginia primary. They burned ballots for them in Texas. Ambassador Joe Kennedy made a deal with crime boss Trafficante and Marcello that the Kennedy administration would drop the Eisenhower administration's attempts to deport those two gangsters.

In fact, the mob was double-crossed as soon as Bobby Kennedy became the Attorney General. He sought to throw both of them out of the country. Their motive is clear. They provide a shooter, maybe two.

Big Texas oil was Lyndon Johnson's big financial patriots. John Kennedy had already announced that he was going to do away with the oil depletion allowance. So, everybody's motive is clear.

Q. You mention the bubble top roof of Kennedy's car.

A. Yes, Bill Moyers[2] gave the order to remove the bubble top from Kennedy's limousine. The bubble top was not bulletproof, but you couldn't see through it. Therefore, Mac Wallace couldn't get the perfect headshot.

Moyers, who did not work for Kennedy, ordered Forrest Vernon Sorrels[3] of the Secret Service in these words, "The President wants that God-damned bubble top removed." The President never said that.

The people who worked for the President all deny giving that order to Moyers. Moyers worked for the Vice President.[4]

Listen to the full interview on my website at

https://www.alanrwarren.com/hom-podcast-episodes/episode/96a687a0/roger-stone-man-who-killed-kennedy-jfk-assassination-series

---

1. **BOBBY BAKER** (Robert Gene Baker) – an American political adviser to Lyndon B. Johnson and an organizer for the Democratic Party. He became the Senate's Secretary to the Majority Leader. In 1963, he resigned during an investigation by the Democratic-controlled Senate into Baker's business and political activities. The investigation included allegations of bribery and arranging sexual favors in exchange for Congressional votes and government contracts. The Senate investigation looked into the financial activities of Baker and Lyndon Johnson during the 1950s. In September 1963, an investigation was begun by the Republican-led Senate Rules Committee into

Baker's business and political activities. Baker was investigated for allegations of bribery using money allocated by Congress and arranging sexual favors in exchange for votes and government contracts. Under increasing criticism, Baker resigned as Secretary to the Majority Leader on October 7, 1963. The investigation of Lyndon Johnson as part of the Baker investigation was later dropped after President Kennedy's assassination and Johnson's ascension to the presidency. *(https://en.wikipedia.org/wiki/Bobby_Baker)*

2. **BILL MOYERS** (Billy Don Moyers) – an American journalist and political commentator. He served as the ninth White House Press Secretary under the Johnson administration from 1965 to 1967. He also worked as a network TV news commentator for ten years. Moyers has been extensively involved with public broadcasting, producing documentaries and news journal program. During the Kennedy Administration, Moyers was first appointed as associate director of public affairs for the newly created Peace Corps in 1961. When Lyndon B. Johnson took office after the Kennedy assassination, Moyers became a special assistant to Johnson, serving from 1963 to 1967. Moyers acted as the President's informal chief of staff from October 1964 until 1966. From July 1965 to February 1967, he also served as White House press secretary. *(https://en.wikipedia.org/wiki/Billy_Don_Moyers*
3. **FORREST VERNON SORRELS** began working for the United States Secret Service on July 6, 1923, as a clerk in the El Paso office. Shortly after, Sorrels began to assist with investigative work, and in 1926, he was appointed as an operative. Later that same year, the agent in charge was transferred, so Sorrels took over the position until 1935. He was then transferred to Dallas as Special Agent in charge but was transferred again to New Orleans the following year as Acting Supervising Agent of a newly

created joint headquarters for Texas, Louisiana, and Mississippi. This headquarters office was then moved to Houston in 1938 and Dallas in 1941, with Sorrels moving with it each time. The headquarters' organization was then disbanded, and the supervising officers were relocated to local offices or to Washington, DC. Forrest Sorrels was placed as Special Agent in Charge of the Dallas district, where he continued through to the time of JFK's assassination in 1963. On November 4, 1963, the Dallas Secret Service office was notified of President Kennedy's trip to Dallas, Texas, later that month. As Special Agent in Charge, Forrest Sorrels had to work closely with DC Secret Service and Dallas Police to begin planning for the trip. After announcing on November 16 that there would be a Presidential motorcade through the city of Dallas, Sorrels became heavily involved in the planning of the route for the motorcade. By November 21, 1963, at 8:00 a.m., the route had been published in the *Dallas Morning News*.

4. **BUBBLE TOP REPORT** – Love Field that day had an outdoor phone line connected to the desk of the *Dallas Times Herald*. A local reporter used it to phone in stories about the scheduled motorcade. Here is the published account by the on-site reporter:

   Just before the plane was scheduled to leave Fort Worth for the short flight to Dallas, Stan Weinberg asked me if the bubble top was going to be on the Presidential limousine. It would help to know now, he said, before he wrote the story later under pressure. It had been raining early that morning, and there was some uncertainty about it. I told Stan that I would find it. I put the phone down and walked over to a small ramp where the motorcade limousines were being held in waiting. I spotted Forrest Sorrels, the agent in charge of the Dallas Secret Service office. I knew Mr. Sorrels fairly well because I was then the regular federal beat reporter. I looked down the ramp. The bubble top was on the President's car.

"Rewrite wants to know if the bubble top's going to stay on," I said to Mr. Sorrels, a man of fifty or so who wore dignified glasses and resembled a preacher or bank president.

He looked at the sky and then hollered over at one of his agents, holding a two-way radio in his hand, "What about the weather downtown?"

The agent talked into his radio for a few seconds, then listened. "Clear," he hollered back.

Mr. Sorrels yelled back at the agents standing by the car, "Take off the bubble top!"

(https://www.lewrockwell.com/2003/11/gary-north/lee-harvey-oswald-was-a-communist/)

Mac Wallace

INTERVIEW WITH JOAN MELLEN

We had the pleasure to interview the next author a couple of times. She is a professor and excellent researcher that only goes with the facts, something we seem to miss out on a lot these days. Joan Mellen talked about a person that many say was Kennedy's primary shooter from the Texas Schoolbook Depository, Mac Wallace.[1]

Joan Mellen is a professor of English and creative writing at Temple University in Philadelphia. She is the author of twenty-four books, ranging from film criticism to fiction, sports, true crime, Latin American studies, and biography. She has written for a variety of publications such as the *New York Times*, the *Los Angeles Times*, and the *Philadelphia*

Inquirer, including the *Baltimore Sun,* where she is a frequent contributor.[2] This interview was from 2018.

Q. What was your purpose in writing this book?

A. I wanted to write a biography on Jim Garrison, whom I had met. The only way I could think of to get through the morass of controversy because there were so many attacks on Jim Garrison was to find out everything I could. The National Archives, after the *JFK* film by Oliver Stone, had the FBI, the CIA, and other agencies release their records on the Kennedy assassination. So, I had to go look at everything and see what was actually there. What were the Garrison files like? What kind of interviews did they do, and with whom?

Q. So, why is there such a negative impression about Jim Garrison?

A. Well, you know that the CIA has media assets? They have people that work for them that express their point of view. One of them was about Garrison, Richard Helm, who in 1967 was the Director of Central Intelligence. He came up with the view that Garrison was being manipulated by the KGB, and that's why he was accusing Shaw.

I found a document from the CIA review group, which stated, "Clay Shaw was a highly paid asset of the CIA." They admitted it in the papers they sent to the House Select Committee. Garrison, when he started to look in the summer of '63 in New Orleans, he saw Oswald roaming around there, and he was never alone. Everyone he was with was in the CIA. Ever since then, Garrison was on their list.

The footprints of the CIA are everywhere in the New Orleans story. That's why when I came to Texas, and I was working on Mac Wallace and Lyndon Johnson, I knew some of the people around the Texas story. There's a big CIA footprint in the JFK assassination, so it couldn't just have been Texas.

Q. Is it hard to find real evidence?

A. I have to tell you something, these are very trying times. Society is being destabilized in a rapid way. I'm teaching at a University, and I had a woman get up in class and issue a tirade of venomous obscenities against women, against gays, and against people who criticize Trump. We were all frightened.

The University has no mechanism to punish a student that does this. Anything goes these days. The social order is falling apart, and in keeping with that, we have this undermining of the research into the Kennedy assassination. That means that people will make up lies; they'll say someone else is a liar, say things like "it's Texas justice," for example, and LBJ did, and there's no proof of that whatsoever.

Jim Garrison wasn't afraid. He went out and did his investigations. They got him finally, though, undermining him through harassment. He lost the office of District Attorney, so he couldn't conduct his investigations any longer. Then he became ill and died fairly young.

Q. What can you tell us about the relationship between Lyndon Johnson and Mac Wallace?

A. Most people think that Mac Wallace was a killer, who killed people for Johnson, Billy Sol Estes, and that whole crowd.

When I started looking into it, I looked at it as if I knew nothing. I found out that he was a young liberal fellow who was an outstanding student at the University of Texas. Johnson liked to pick out people like that to come to his office and work for him, and Mac Wallace was only one of many. Another one we know was Bill Moyer. John Connally was one. They were usually all from the University of Texas.

The killer myth was created by Billy Sol Estes, a petty criminal who was finally caught in various scams. When he was caught, he thought Johnson would protect him. But Johnson distanced himself, fast. So, Billy Sol Estes went to jail.

When Billy Sol Estes got out after his second term in jail, in 1984 or '85, he went to a grand jury and accused Lyndon Johnson of organizing the murder of a person that worked for the Agriculture Department called Henry Marshall. He claimed that Mac Wallace was hired by Johnson to kill Marshall. Henry Marshall was murdered, and so were several people who had worked for Billy Sol Estes. Marshall did not work for Sol Estes. He was the one who was going to report him. Then later, Mac Wallace was accused of many other murders. He was even accused by Billy Sol Estes of killing Johnson's sister. Then to top it all off, it would be Kennedy.

It turned out that one of these zealous but sincere researchers, Jay Harrison, got a bee in his bonnet about Mac Wallace. There was one unidentified fingerprint from the Texas Schoolbook Depository, and it was in the hands of the Warren Commission, who got it from the FBI after the Kennedy assassination.

Jay got the idea it belonged to Mac Wallace. So, he hired a forensics examiner to look at the fingerprint and look at Wallace's. Mac Wallace had killed somebody in the 1950s during a crime of passion, a golf professional named Kinser, and so his fingerprints had been taken then.

Mac Wallace had also joined the marines in 1939, and they had his fingerprints as well. But Jay didn't have the Navy's print. You can only get them after a number of years, and they hadn't passed for him, but they did for me.

The police prints were a little bit blurred because they hadn't cleaned off the machine from the previous perpetrator. The examiner was convinced it was Mac Wallace, though.

So, I got an examiner from the office that certifies Fingerprint Examiners, and I gave him the Navy print and the police print.

Then, I got the print from the Warren Commission from the National Archives.

My examiner said that the print from the Navy and the print from the police are the same people. But the one from the Texas Schoolbook Depository is not that person.

So, all of these authors went ballistic because their theories that Johnson was behind it and using Mac Wallace all came from that fingerprint.

When I told Mac Wallace's kids, his son was relieved because he knew he was at home with his father the day of the assassination. Also, because of the black mark on the state of Texas.

Q. So, is there any truth to Wallace being the hitman for Johnson?

A. No. He did do some jobs for Johnson like a lot of other young men. Johnson took a lot of these young men, and he used them and destroyed their lives.

Listen to the full interview on my website at

https://www.alanrwarren.com/hom-podcast-episodes/episode/bd4cb5bf/joan-mellen-faustian-bargains-jfk-assassination-series

---

1. **MAC WALLACE** (Malcolm Everett Wallace) – an economist for the United States Department of Agriculture and served as a press secretary for President Lyndon B. Johnson. On October 22, 1951, Wallace fatally shot John Douglas Kinser in the clubhouse of an Austin golf course owned by Kinser. The prosecution did not attempt to establish a motive for the shooting, nor did it produce an eyewitness to it or the murder weapon. The jury returned its verdict finding Wallace guilty of "murder with malice." After a short recess, O'Betts sentenced Wallace to a five-year sentence that was suspended. Wallace is most widely known for his alleged participation in the assassination of President John F. Kennedy in Dallas, Texas, on November 22, 1963. *(https://peoplepill.com/people/malcolm-mac-wallace/, https://en.wikipedia.org/wiki/Malcolm_%22Mac%22_Wallace)*
2. About the Author | JOAN MELLEN. *http://joanmellen.com/wordpress/about-the-author/*

The Recordings

INTERVIEW WITH MAX HOLLAND

During the past years and talking with quite a few authors about the Kennedy assassination, one thing that seemed to be consistent was the reports about the White House recordings surrounding Lyndon Johnson. I had never listened to them, so I thought that was the next step to take. It would also be appropriate to discuss the recordings with the journalist who covered them enough to write a book and do a documentary about them, Max Holland.

Max Holland is an American journalist, author, and editor of *Washington Decoded,* an internet newsletter on US history that began publishing on March 11, 2007. He is currently a contributing editor to the *Nation* and the *Wilson Quarterly* and sits on the International Journal of Intelligence and Counterintelligence editorial advisory board. As of 2004, he had more than two decades of journalism experience. His articles have appeared in the *Atlantic Monthly, American Heritage,* the *Washington Post,* the *New York Times,* the *Los Angeles Times,* the *Boston Globe,* the *Baltimore Sun, Studies in Intelligence, The Journal of Cold War Studies, Reviews in American History,* and online at *History News Network.*

Holland's published books include *Leak: Why Mark Felt Became Deep Throat* (University Press of Kansas, 2012), *The Kennedy Assassination Tapes: The White House Conversations of Lyndon B. Johnson Regarding the Assassination, The Warren Commission,* and *The Aftermath* (Knopf, 2004), *The CEO Goes to Washington: Negotiating the Halls of Power* (Whittle Direct Books, 1994), and *When the Machine Stopped: A Cautionary Tale from Industrial America* (Harvard Business School Press, 1989). In 2011, he was the lead consultant for a *National Geographic* television documentary about the Kennedy assassination that premiered in November 2011, entitled *JFK: The Lost Bullet.* The findings of the documentary were summarized in

The DeRonja-Holland Report.[1] Holland appeared on our show in early 2019.

Q. Max, you actually have the tapes of Lyndon Johnson, which covers the time after the assassination of Kennedy. How did you obtain them?

A. Well, it was after Oliver Stone's movie *JFK*. Congress passed legislation mandating the gathering and release of all assassination-related documents, and one of the documents was the tapes that Lyndon Johnson made while he was President. These were technically exempt from the legislation because they were under a deed of "gift" from Johnson to his own library and closed for 75 years. However, the library director, a fellow named Harry Milton, thought it would be a good idea to open them. So, with the permission of Lady Bird Johnson, they exhumed the tapes, which had never been heard.

At first, they started out with all of the assassination-related tapes. These were tapes made the day of and the days immediately after the assassination, leading up to the Warren Commission's creation. Then there were a lot of assassination-related conversations in December, but gradually it became less and less a topic. Then, it was just a smattering of conversations in January, March, and April.

Later in 1966 and '67, the assassination rears its head again with Jim Garrison and other critics of the Warren Report. Eventually, Harry Middleton persuaded Lady Bird to release all of the Johnson tapes on any subject. Those were heard on *C-Span*, and a lot of people find them entertaining and informative. But in 2004, I put out a book just looking at these assassination-related tapes and trying to put them in context.

One of the things about these tapes is that they are so orientated to the events of the day that unless you have enough context, you can literally misunderstand them.

Q. When Lyndon Johnson talks on these tapes about the assassination, he doesn't talk as if he is behind it or knows what happened. Wouldn't that in itself eliminate the books that have been put out by people like Roger Stone that accuses Johnson of being behind the murder of Kennedy?

A. Yes. But I'm sure Stone already has an answer to that. You know, like the tapes were made on purpose to confuse the historical issue or culpability of Johnson. The answer to your question is yes, but like our President (Donald Trump), he will say anything.

Q. What's the tone of Johnson on the tapes?

A. If you listen to them, Johnson is desperate for information. He's concerned about whether he's a target too. He doesn't know if this is an attempt to decapitate the American Government, whether by Cuba or the Soviet Union. To any reasonable person, it's clear that they exculpate Johnson.

Q. What's your assessment of the Warren Commission report?

A. I'm kind of in the middle. I started out sort of agnostic. I didn't know what to make of the Commission.

Before I researched it, I was concerned that they didn't know this, and they didn't do that. The FBI withheld information from them. Robert Kennedy withheld information from them. The CIA withheld information from them. How good of a job could they have done when they were denied all of this information?

But then, as I got into the case, I'd say it became known and admitted that I was a staunch defender of the integrity of the Commission. I've interviewed almost all of the staff members. I interviewed Gerald Ford before he died; he was the last remaining Commissioner.

So, I'm a staunch defender of its basic integrity. But it's also true that the Commission made mistakes that put its own work in disrepute. I'll admit to that.

Q. Such as?

A. The biggest one to my way of thinking, is that they accepted the widespread reception that the "Zapruder film"[2] was an actual recording of the entire assassination. Because they did that, they made some big mistakes that injured their reputation.

Q. One thing I hear a lot is because Allen Dulles, head of the CIA, was fired by President Kennedy, he should not have been on the Warren Commission. What do you think?

A. Well, if you listen to the conversation between Johnson and Dulles, at that time, it was known that Oswald had gone to Mexico and gone to the Cuban and Soviet Embassies. It was considered an intelligence issue of the highest order that suggested perhaps because it had happened just weeks before the assassination, there was some connection between the communists and the assassination.

So, Johnson wanted one of America's most esteemed intelligence experts on the Commission.

Dulles didn't want to go on it because he was afraid of the propaganda windfall from the Soviet Union if he was on the Commission. He knew they were going to accuse him of being part of an intelligence whitewash. So, he says, "Are you sure you want me to do this, Mr. President? Have you thought through all of the implications?"

Johnson wasn't going to take no for an answer, so he put Dulles on. Dulles knew that it made for propaganda that the head of the CIA was on this. It was just going to give Soviet propaganda a real theme to mine: Dulles was engaged in a real intelligence cover-up.

Of course, some people believe that he did. But the only thing that he helped cover-up, from my point of view, was that we had been trying to kill Castro. But Robert Kennedy was covering that up too.

Q. But it was eventually going to come out, correct?

A. Yes, but in how long? Ten years, 20 years, or even 50 years. Certainly, they didn't foresee what was going to happen. I mean, it really came out because of Watergate. That's when it was really confirmed. There were newspaper reports of it before, that's to be sure. But it's different having a newspaper story or columnist just alleging it than having the U.S. government and CIA witnesses testify to it. They were operating on the fact that it needed to be kept secret, and they certainly weren't going to step forward and be the first to break that secret.

Q. You tell us in your book that Oswald's first shot was missed. What do you mean by that?

A. Well, that point is related to the Zapruder film. What happened was that after Oswald was murdered two days after the assassination, the overwhelming vantage point for the assassination shifted from his sniper's perch on the sixth floor of the Texas Schoolbook Depository to the Zapruder film. That shift took place because the Zapruder film was the only record of the shooting. If it hadn't been made, we would have had to stick with re-staging the assassination from Oswald's point of view. But instead, the presumption was made that Zapruder had recorded the assassination in full.

If you look at the Zapruder film, it's 26 seconds in duration. The first seven seconds are just of the motorcycles, the lead motorcycles driving by. Zapruder stopped his camera after about seven seconds of running it because, in those days, you had a wind-up camera. He didn't know exactly how much film he had left, and he didn't want to record Dallas motorcycle policeman.

So, he waited until he saw the President.

As soon as he was sure that he was seeing the President, he started his camera, and that's frame 133. Then it rolls until the end. Well, if you actually think about it for a while, you realize that the car, the limousine was already about 70 feet down into Dealey Plaza by that time.

Oswald, a marine trained to fire at the upper body mass, and we've all seen those silhouettes, the head, and the upper body torso, that's what he was trained to fire at. That silhouette came into his line of sight about 1.7 seconds before Zapruder restarted his camera.

I suddenly realized that Oswald had his target in sight before Zapruder started his camera again, and I realized that there was a possibility of a fundamental misunderstanding. One in which Zapruder's perspective was equated with Oswald's, when, in fact, they were two different perspectives.

Through that, I realized that in all likelihood, and the best explanation of what happened was that Oswald fired before Zapruder restarted his camera.

So, you're never going to find the first shot, which people were looking for in the

Zapruder film because it already happened. The Zapruder film only makes sense when you realize it was the second and third shots. This whole business of whether Oswald had enough time, how difficult it was, etc., etc., is all put to rest when you realize that.

In fact, if you look at Zapruder's testimony before the Warren Commission, he says, "I heard two shots. They say there were three. I'm not going to say that there are not three, but I heard and saw two shots." That's what he filmed, and that's all he filmed.

So, all these "six seconds" in Dallas, and how could someone operate a rifle that quickly, that all melts away when you realize that the film is a time clock of the assassination, yes, but it's of a clock that already started. The film is one that was extremely informative, but it was also extremely deceptive because it became the vision of the assassination.

You couldn't imagine the assassination without running the film in your head, when in fact, the film was only partial.

Q. So, explain the shots for us.

A. The first shot that hit him was the second shot. The first shot didn't hit him and didn't hit anybody. That's another issue. Why did it miss? For the moment, let's just put that aside.

The second shot was the one that hit him in the upper back, exited his throat, and hit Connally.

The third shot was the one that hit him in the head. Those last two were the two shots Zapruder says he noticed and filmed.

Q. Why is it so important for people to find out all the details behind the JFK assassination?

A. We have these periodic eruptions of interest in the JFK case because it was never truly put to rest. It took me a long time to come to this analytical point of view.

You know, the Warren Commission had five questions to answer. Two of them were already answered before they even started work: What happened? The assassination of the President, and when did it happen? Everybody knew that. But the other questions needed answers: who, how, and why.

Now, the 'how' was going to determine who, right? Once you figure out how exactly he was killed, that would point the finger at who. And who is going to tell you why? Well, since one of the "who's" was killed right away, you're left to speculate. Your analysis of Oswald's motive is as good as mine, or as good as anybody else's. He left no note. He didn't explain himself to his brother or his wife. So, it's really a matter of interpreting his past and coming to your own conclusion about that. So, that goes to motive. Even if he physically did the killing in Dealey Plaza, did he have any confederates outside who were assisting him, or put him up to it, or going to help him to get away? Again, his murder leaves that vaguer than we want.

So, that leaves how. How was the President murdered in Dealey Plaza? That was a question I thought the Warren Commission could have and should have answered in a clear, compelling, and concise way. Because of the problem with the Zapruder film, believing that all three shots fired were on the film in some way, if you read the pages in the Warren Report, I wouldn't say that it's inaccurate, but it's the most convoluted, confusing explanation because they go through each of the possibilities.

The first shot fired was the one that missed. The second shot fired was the one that missed, or the third shot fired was the one that missed. Initially, they thought what made the most sense was that the third shot fired was the one that missed because the car would be furthest away and, of course, would be the most likely to miss. But almost everybody in Dealey Plaza said that the shot to the head was the last. So, that didn't work.

Conversely, if you know you hit him twice with those distances, how could he miss when he was closest? That didn't seem to make sense either, superficially. However, it's a more difficult shot than you might think.

So, they kind of said that it was the second shot that missed. Once you do that, you're in these three shots in six seconds and of a moving target, and it becomes exceedingly difficult to do that. Not impossible but difficult, and it just opened a can of worms that the Warren Commission never successfully put an end to.

Once you start questioning the how, well, the who, and the why are, as I said, problematic to begin with. So, if you haven't even answered the how, and there's only one way it happened, it doesn't happen a different way every time you see the President drive through Dealey Plaza. It happened one way. Well, which was that one way?

They didn't come up with that because, basically, they ran out of time. They had a lot to do. They came up with one shot hitting both men, which was true, but a departure from what the FBI had found. They thought they had done a good job. In fact, it was a soft underbelly.

Q. Was the rifle a problem as he couldn't reload it fast enough?

A. There's a lot of issues that are involved in that. It was a bolt action rifle, not an automatic rifle, where you pull the trigger and squeeze off three shots in a blink of an eye. So, there's a lot of factors that go into it.

But I've worked on it for a long time, and basically, it came down to what I think is the rock bottom truth: the "how" was the question that they should have answered. They shouldn't have rested until they had the answer. There was an answer. It was elusive, and they didn't get it. You can't say that the report is wrong if you read it. It was written by lawyers, and you practically have to be a lawyer to read it. But you can't say the language is wrong. It's not as clear as it should have been.

Critics, some of whom were not well-intentioned, have exploited that fact to the Commission's detriment. You can't blame the critics. It's the Commission's fault.

Listen to the full interview on my website at

https://www.alanrwarren.com/hom-podcast-episodes/episode/b3baaa7c/max-holland-kennedy-assassination-tapes

---

1. **MAX HOLLAND** – Wikipedia. *https://en.wikipedia.org/wiki/Max_Holland*
2. **THE ZAPRUDER FILM** – a silent 8mm color motion picture sequence shot by Abraham Zapruder with a home-movie camera, as U.S. President John F. Kennedy's motorcade passed through Dealey Plaza in Dallas, Texas, on November 22, 1963. Unexpectedly, it ended up capturing the President's assassination. *(https://en.wikipedia.org/wiki/Zapruder_film)*

The Other Video Of The Assassination

INTERVIEW WITH GAYLE NIX JACKSON

Another popular event that hit the news about the JFK assassination was the possibility of another man who was in Dallas filming the JFK precession in Dealey Plaza. A man by the name of Orville Nix. Could this "Nix film" be true? So, next up was finding his closest living relative and perhaps viewing the film he took that day. Abraham Zapruder's film gets all the attention, but there was another eyewitness to history whose tale has yet to be told.

In this eye-opening account, Gayle Nix Jackson tells the story of her grandfather, Orville Nix, a man with a camera who happened to be on the ground for a life-changing, world-changing, and in some ways world-ending event: the murder of President Kennedy in Dallas in 1963. This interview took place in the Spring of 2018.

Q. So, your grandfather, Orville Nix, was at Dallas watching the President, and I understand that he had a camera. What kind of camera did he have, a moving picture film type camera or one that just took still shots?

A. It was a film camera.

Q. What was his background?

A. He worked for the General Services Administration[1], which is another government entity. Essentially, he was an air conditioning repair guy, which means that he was the glorified janitor. He had a fourth-grade education as he had to quit school to help his family with money. He had a brother with epilepsy, so he worked his whole life trying to better himself. He tried to educate himself because he couldn't go to school.

Q. Explain what happened that day with your grandfather while at Dealey Plaza.

A. One of the ways he did that was by making friends with people he worked with at the GSA. In this case, it was Errol Morris, a key person in Dealey Plaza that day. He was one of my grandfather's dear friends.

Morris told him early, even before it was in the papers, "Look, Orville, if you want to take your grandkids to see the President, here's the best place to go." So, he made plans for me, my sister, and my brother to go down with my grandmother to see the President.

We were to meet my grandfather there at noon. The crowds were all so large; there were people everywhere. We couldn't make it to get to him. The crowds were too thick. We waited for him at the H.L. Greens.

We saw the motorcade go by, but we weren't there in Dealey Plaza, but my grandfather was, and he took those pictures. He had bought this Keystone camera, and my grandmother, who worked at the cafeteria, was always upset with him because he was spending money on cameras and film. He just thought it was the most wonderful thing to see airplanes flying, and it was high technology to him.

So, he bought this camera just for this event, but he didn't know how to work it well. He used what many of the naysayers from the Warren Commission say when they talk about the Nix tape, specifically, "Orville Nix didn't know what he was doing. He used indoor film."

One of the things I don't ever talk about but should is Roland Zavada. He is the expert for Kodak and does all the speeches about film for them. I have talked to him at length for years, and he said, "Gayle, one thing that you never talk about and I find odd is that your grandfather used indoor film and the Nix film is very dark." If you have seen it, then you will see that it's a dark film. Well, when you use indoor film, and this is logical, it's going to let in more light because it's indoor film. So, really and truly, if you look at the Nix film, you will think that it was over-lit because he used indoor film. But it's not. It's very dark, and that's very strange.

Q. The Nix film gets a lot of attention because of the grassy knoll. Maybe explain that.

A. It's the only film that shows the grassy knoll in its entirety. So, when he scans over the grassy knoll part, it's very dark. You can't see hardly anything. That's odd, at least to Mr. Zavada, the Kodak expert. It shouldn't be that way.

Q. So, why do you think it's that way?

A. I don't know. There are all of these rumors and all of these arguments about alterations, the Zapruder film alterations.

Q. Did he turn the film over to authorities?

A. My grandfather turned it over to the FBI because they had issued an edict saying, "any film showing anything to do with Dealey Plaza must be turned over to the

FBI immediately." So, when my grandfather's film was developed, it was a week after the assassination. He had so much film left on his camera that he didn't want to have it developed until he used more. He didn't even know that he had assassination footage.

Q. So, when he handed in the camera, did your grandfather see something or say something about the film?

A. Yes.

Q. What was his interpretation of what was on the film?

A. Well, when they called him, Dynacolor was the processing plant processing his film. They called him in the middle of the night because they worked all night doing these things. He was a really good customer as he was always spending money on this film and just upset my grandmother. They knew him very well and said, "Mr. Nix, you've got assassination images on your film." He said, "No." He really didn't know that he was taking the film. My grandfather was tall, 6 foot 5 inches, and his keystone camera had a grip on it, kind of like a gun. When he heard the shots ringing out, he clinched that grip, as you would if you were white-knuckling a steering wheel in the rain or the snow.

Because he had it clinched and it was at his waist, as he was running, he got the footage. So, if you ever see a first-generation copy of the Nix film, you will know it is authentic because it looks like the motorcade was going uphill. It wasn't uphill. It was because of the way my grandfather was holding the camera.

When they watched it at Dynacolor, and they probably watched it 30 times, they couldn't believe what they saw and that you could see the assassination. And though it's not as graphic as the Zapruder film, you could still see the plume of blood and the grey matter that occurred at the kill shot, and it's terrible.

He took it to the FBI early the next day, which was a Monday. They told him that they would give it back to him in a day, and they just needed to make a copy of it for themselves. They didn't return it to him for four days.

That has always been a question for our family. Why did they do that? Why would they need to keep it so long? But Americans didn't question their government in those days; they just didn't. It was before Woodstock, before protesters. Maybe later they did, but at that time, if you were a certain age, you just didn't question what the government was doing.

When he got it back from the FBI, he noticed that it was different. I asked him, "How would you know that it's different? You just watched it on a wall. How can you say it's different?" He said, "Because it's jumpy, and because it's darker. Because it's not what I saw."

I said to him, "Maybe it's because you watched it on a wall. Maybe there was something on the wall that made it look weird." He would get really upset then and say, "Look, it was my film, and I know what

I took. I know what I saw, and that is not what I saw."

So, I had always wondered, as many members of my family did, if something happened when the FBI had it. My grandfather was convinced it had. But my thought was that it was illogical. If you were going to alter my grandfather's film, you would also have to alter the Zapruder film.

Q. What did you mean earlier when you mentioned different versions of the film?

A. They had lost my grandfather's camera's original film. There is no original to take to Japan or say to Sweden, where they've got awesome technology now. It could show if there were someone on the grassy knoll. We could see it if we had the camera original, but we don't, because the government lost it.

Q. How did they lose that?

A. Yeah, exactly! How do you? It's evidence in an open murder case, and they lose it.

How does that happen? It doesn't make sense to me. I have been chasing after this film my whole life. I have talked to everyone on the photographic committee of the House Select Committee, but unfortunately, most of them have since passed away. But every one of them told me they never even saw the original film. They only saw frames. Now, how are you going to do a really good job determining what happened that day when you don't have the evidence. It's just a joke. And what is being hidden from us?

Q. Gayle, what do you think that they are hiding?

A. I think that they are hiding somebody on the knoll, that's what I think. My grandfather died in 1972, and until the day he died, he would say the shots changed from the stockade fence. That's what he called it. Now we call it the grassy knoll, and the fence was behind it.

In fact, in 1967, CBS came down, and at that time, my grandfather had been getting weird phone calls and strange people knocking at his door. He was never threatened. I don't want you to think that there was anything nefarious that way. Strange things were happening that he couldn't understand.

The Warren Commission had just closed, and CBS was, of course, wanting to say, "Don't we have a great government? Look what the Warren Commission decided. Lee Harvey Oswald did it on his own." So, they would ask my grandfather, "Mr. Nix, you were one of the men who took film of the assassination. What did you see? Where did the shots come from?" Every time he would say, "Over there by the stockade fence." The director would yell, "Cut cut cut!" This went on two or three different times.

By the fourth time, the man who was the director, came over to my grandfather and said, "Mr. Nix, where did the Warren Commission say the shots came from?" Well, they said it came from over there at the schoolbook depository by that skinny little communist." The director said, "Well, okay, that's what you need to say." Then that's what he said because that's what they told him he needed to say.

Q. Why can't they both be true?

A. I totally agree with you. I believe there was more than one shooter. I have never believed Lee Harvey Oswald did this alone. But I'm also one of those people that doesn't believe he was innocent. I don't think he was a hero; I think he knew exactly what he was into, and maybe he got in there a little too deep. But I don't think he did this alone. I think the assassination and the cover-up are two separate entities. I don't think they went hand in hand. I think the assassination happened and put whoever was in charge, and I have no idea who was in charge. I think there was some sort of rogue element, and it caught them off guard. So, they had to come up with an answer quickly as to what was going on because they were scared that we would blame Russians or Cubans, and we would go into World War III.

Q. What do you think your grandfather's film contradicts about the Warren Commission results?

A. My grandfather said there were more than three shots. He thought there were four or five, and two of them happened, one right after the other. Like BMA, pause, BAM, pause, BAM BAM! That's how he heard it.

Q. He is not the first to say that. But it has been said that it was the echo that caused that.

A. Right, Dealey Plaza is a lot like New Orleans. It's like an upside-down bowl, so it does echo. But if you're there and you're dive-bombing into the ground, like all of those people were, they know what they heard. And why would we not listen to those people?

Q. Did your grandfather testify to anybody about what he heard?

A. No, he was never called into the Warren Commission to testify. They had him go to the FBI to give his report to a couple of guys there. How could you take a film of the JFK assassination and not be testifying in front of the Warren Commission?

Listen to the full interview on my website at

> https://www.alanrwarren.com/hom-podcast-episodes/episode/d4d7c15f/gayle-nix-jackson-missing-jfk-assassination-tape

---

1. **GENERAL SERVICES ADMINISTRATION** (GSA) – provides workplaces by constructing, managing, and preserving government buildings and by leasing and managing commercial real estate. GSA's acquisition solutions offer private sector professional services, equipment, supplies, and IT to government organizations and the military. GSA also promotes management best practices and efficient government operations through the development of governmentwide policies. *(https://www.gsa.gov/about-us)*

The Central Intelligence Agency

INTERVIEW WITH JOHN KOERNER

At this point in my investigation, it was time for me to go deeper into the theory of the CIA's involvement in the assassination. The person I interviewed next had released a book, *Why the CIA Killed JFK and Malcolm X: The Secret Drug Trade in Laos.* John Koerner is a professor of American History at Erie Community College in Williamsville, N.Y. He is the author of several books about the paranormal, including *The Mysteries of Father Baker, The Father Baker Code, Supernatural Power, The Secret Plot to Kill McKinley,* and *Why the CIA Killed JFK and Malcolm X: The Secret Drug Trade in Laos.* Koerner has a master's degree in American History from The State University of

New York, College at Brockport, and a bachelor's degree in Communication and Journalism from St. John Fisher College, where he graduated summa cum laude with Honors. He is also the founder of *Paranormal Walks (paranormalwalks.com)*, a ghost walk company that explores the paranormal history of Western New York through annual walking tours. He resides with his family in Buffalo, New York.

Q. Do you think that Lee Harvey Oswald was the person who shot the President, or was he even a part of it, or a patsy?

A. It seemed like from my perspective, he was a patsy. Which even by his own admission said he was. When you look at some of the evidence behind this, I think one interesting way to point at the evidence is from a man E. Howard Hunt.

Hunt was an agent in the CIA from almost the very beginning to the end of his life, and he gave a death bed confession to his son. In that confession, he talked about an extensive plot to kill President Kennedy, and he named a number of different names, including himself. A lot of this stuff has checked out since his confession.

A number of people interested in keeping the drug trade going were involved in the assassination to kill President Kennedy. Including a man named David Morales and other men too. So, it seems from the evidence put forward, that's where it comes from.

My book isn't so much about who killed Kennedy; it's more about sort of why Kennedy was killed. The motive was to keep the drug trade going in Southeast Asia because there was so much money to be made off it.

Q. So, you're following the money here and suggesting it's more about the money that the drug trade made. Are you saying the CIA was running the drug operation and collecting the money?

A. Right. In fact, since the book came out, I've had a number of different men contact me, and they've talked about how they were involved in it directly. They're thankful that the truth is finally coming out. Some work has been done already about this. For example, Gary Webb was writing about how the agency was involved in the drug trade in South America. There's a film about him now called *Kill the Messenger* when he died mysteriously back in 2004. Another man named Louis Lomax was writing about this back in the 1960s. He was a TV reporter too. He also died mysteriously in 1970. So, there's been some writing about this and some discussion. But those who have talked about it have paid an enormous price, including death in some cases.

Q. Are the files still sealed around the JFK assassination?

A. Yes, a number of them are. Let's mention David Morales, as there are 61 sealed files for him. E. Howard Hunt said that this guy was directly involved in the assassination of President Kennedy. He even admitted it to many of his friends that he was there in Dallas. He was also at the scene of the Howard Keyes assassination, too, at the Ambassador Hotel in the Embassy Ballroom. He admitted that he was there to kill Robert Kennedy. So, this is one man of many whose files are sealed. There's probably a lot of things in there that would implicate these people directly in the assassination – just talking about the men E. Howard Hunt named to assassinate President Kennedy. There are 123 pages and files on William K. Harvey, yet to be released, 606 files on David Atlee Phillips, 232 pages, and files on E. Howard Hunt that they haven't released yet, and there are also 61 files on David Morales.

Q. Okay, the assassination of JFK, was it just so they could continue running drugs?

A. Let's just put this in some perspective. There was so much money they were making in the drug trade. For example, one week in November 1963, when the President was killed, the agency shipped 1,146 kilos of opium to South Vietnam, and that netted them a profit of $97,000. Just for that one shipment, one month, in one year. So, enormous amounts of cash were available to them to be made.

Laos was called the golden triangle in Southeast Asia. As long as they could justify fighting communism in that country, they could stay there. One key thing to this was Vietnam. To them, Vietnam was a big marketplace for heroin to sell to the men fighting the war there. As long as they kept the war going, they kept growing, selling, and trading drugs. Money men have emailed me since the book came out and said, "Yes, we have actually bought heroin from agents of the CIA." Many of them needed heroin because the combat was so stressful for them. Many of them, we're talking hundreds of thousands of men, came home from Vietnam addicted to heroin. We know that 60,000 have killed themselves since the Vietnam war ended. So, it's really all tied in.

Q. Was JFK just not popular with the CIA and military?

A. There was resistance from the military and the CIA because he refused to go to war in Cuba, Laos, and Vietnam. Those that wanted war, to fight communism, and keep the drugs going were just bitterly opposed to him. One thing the agency did that was just diabolical to get back at him for his peace policies was they tried to destroy the Peace Corp. They attempted this by pretending they were college students and not agents in the CIA. So, they're trying to use JFK's Peace Corp. for war. It was like trying to kill Mister Rogers. How bad can you get? If you ever go to the Peace Corp website, it says, "If you've ever been in the CIA, you can't ever be in the Peace Corp. Don't even bother to apply."

Q. JFK also had his own problems with the CIA. Didn't he fire some of them?

A. Yes. We can start with the Bay of Pigs Invasion. The attempts to remove Fidel Castro, which went horribly wrong. The agency told him that if we sent in 1500 men to Cuba, we'd get rid of Castro. Well, it didn't work. The invasion completely failed, and they got captured, tortured, and killed. But during the invasion, the CIA told Kennedy to bomb Cuba or invade them. He said no, we're not going to do that as they pose no threat to us, and that would start a third world war with Russia.

From that point forward, they began to split. They thought he was soft on communism, and he thought they were hellbent on war. So, as you said, he fired Allen Dulles, the Director. He fired Richard Bissell, the Director of Operations. He fired Capo, another man in the agency. So, these different events were kind of like house cleaning events.

Then, the following summer of 1961, he signed NSAN 51, 52, and 53, which basically moved the agency's covert operations to the Joint Chiefs of Staff, taking away almost all of their power. That began his effort as he said to break them into a thousand pieces.

Q. Did the Cuban Missile Crisis have anything to do with the assassination?

A. The Cuban Missile Crisis happened, and he solved it peacefully in October of '62. From that point forward, he enjoyed enormous levels of popularity. There was a poll from the Spring of 1963 that pitted him against Barry Goldwater for the election of 1964. He just tromped him, so the public liked him. But there were groups that didn't like him too, like in the south and the military. So, it was pretty clear that there was going to be four more years of JFK. That was just not acceptable if you were in the agency or in the military because of his consistent efforts at peace in Southeast Asia. He did set out to withdraw from the Vietnam War and wanted to have that done by 1965. That would have stopped the agency from being able to sell drugs to the soldiers in Southeast Asia.

Q. What about the rumors that JFK wasn't going to have Lyndon Johnson as his Vice President in his second term?

A. Yes, that was another possibility. In fact, ironically, Richard Nixon said in Dallas the night before the assassination that they were not going to have Lyndon Johnson on the ticket. And the President had said it privately to some people as well, that he was thinking about changing Johnson. E. Howard Hunt mentioned that Johnson was directly involved and had knowledge of the conspiracy to assassinate President Kennedy. So, if he were thinking of removing him, of course, it would give Johnson more motive to be involved in the whole operation.

Q. So, was Johnson involved?

A. It's obvious in some ways that Johnson had a clear motive to do this. We can go back to the drug trade too. The agency knew very well that Johnson was much more in favor of promoting and expanding the CIA's access to drugs in Southeast Asia, and they would get that from him directly when he became President. There certainly was motive there for him, and the evidence exists that they talked, and before the assassination, they gave him intelligence for the assassination. They were letting him know what was happening in Southeast

Asia. So, they knew his perspective even before the assassination took place. We also know that the day after they bury President Kennedy, Johnson signed Nation Security Referendum 273, which reversed JFK's withdrawal policy and expanded the agency's covert operations in Southeast Asia.

Q. Why was Laos so important for the CIA?

A. The Joint Chiefs of Staff recommended to President Kennedy that we fight the war in Southeast Asia and Laos. We could have won the war on communism there. To do this, they needed to commit 60,000 ground troops. JFK said that we couldn't win there. Our military wasn't equipped to fight in jungles and tunnels. We fought in land battles. He thought we would be bogged down there for years and that it would never work. He was proven right. The Joint Chiefs kept pushing him and even tried to trick him because they knew that 60,000 ground troops meant 60,000 more customers for them to sell heroin to.

Q. How did they try and trick him?

A. Once we get to 1962, the President felt that he wanted to try and get peace in Laos, from communist to anti-communist, stop the drug trade, and stop the war. And he got the job done. He got a peace settlement in Laos, with help from Khrushchev from Russia. It was a great victory for him and his administration.

So, if this were going to work, he had to make sure that there were men in the new Laos government that he could trust. He got them in place, but within a few months, the agency assassinated them. Other men formed a new government. That was one big step towards war when they killed the men who supported JFK in Laos. As long as war went on in Laos, the agency could justify being there.

There was an anti-communist army in Laos, the Royal Lao Army, that JFK supported. The agency, at one point in time, tried to destroy that army. They tried to trick JFK into sending ground troops into Southeast Asia. They thought that if they destroyed that army, they could trick JFK into going to war, like with the Bay of Pigs invasion. But in both cases, he said we're still not going to go to war, and we're still going to resist invading Laos.

Q. You say in your book that the CIA was also behind the murder of Martin Luther King. Tell us about that.

A. There's a book called *An Act of State* by William Pepper that talked a lot about this and really proved the agency was behind it. The part that interested me the most, though, and connected to my thesis was about a guy named Doug Valentine. He wrote a book in 1990, where he talked about how the assassins for Dr. King were from something called "Operation Phoenix." Operation Phoenix was used by the CIA to keep the Vietnam War and its drug trade going as long as possible. One man in Operation Phoenix was David Morales. I mentioned before that Morales was picked by Hunt as one of JFK's assassins. So, we can connect the assassinations.

Q. You also connect the assassination of RFK. Was his assassination just to stop him from becoming the President, or was it because he, too, would shut down the CIA?

A. You're right on both points. With Robert Kennedy, he was so devastated by his brother's death that he even started to wear his brother's clothing to feel closer to him. He even sometimes went to the cemetery where his brother was buried and slept there overnight, next to the eternal flame. He was *that* devastated by the death of his brother. He actually bribed the guards at the cemetery to let him in for the night. He would bring his sleeping bag and sleep next to his brother's grave. On the day of the assassination, he went to the agency's Director John Cohen and told him I know you did this, and I'm going to prove it.

So, he spent the next several years trying to prove the agency killed his brother. He concluded that they did it, and one thing he wanted to do if he became President was to expose the truth of the assassination. He wanted to bring those who did this to trial and execute them for treason. He wanted to dismantle the agency. So, if he became President, that would be the end of the CIA. To them, that was a huge threat.

January of 1968 was a key month for this whole story. That year was kind of a changing year for the agency. They wanted to move access to drugs into the United States. They wanted to expand the domestic drug market. They had done so before, but they wanted more access to it. So, that month the agency arranged a meeting, or Morales did. Morales was one of the men involved. He arranged a meeting between Santo Trafficante with the drug suppliers in Vietnam. The purpose of the meeting was to plan how they could expand the drug trade into the United States and the western hemisphere.

A few months later, the agency assassinated Doctor King and also Robert Kennedy as part of the plan to expand the drug trade. One of the things they did was to use the coffin of a dead soldier from Vietnam as a way to ship the drugs from Southeast Asia to the United States. They even cut open a body and stashed bags of heroin or opium in the body cavities. They filled up as much of the box as they could and shipped it to the United States.

Listen to the full interview on my website at

> https://www.alanrwarren.com/hom-podcast-episodes/episode/b4d3a66d/joe-koerner-why-the-cia-killed-jfk-jfk-assassination-series

The Secret Service

INTERVIEW WITH VINCENT PALAMARA

To find out just what the Secret Service was all about, and if they had something to do with the assassination, either through planning or their inaction during the killing of the President, I would have to go to the expert on the Secret Service. Vincent Palamara is the leading civilian Secret Service authority and the author of 5 books: *Survivor's Guilt: The Secret Service & the Failure to Protect President Kennedy* (2013), *JFK: From Parkland to Bethesda – the Ultimate Kennedy Assassination Compendium* (2015), *The Not So Secret Service – Agency Tales from FDR to the Kennedy Assassination to the Reagan* (2017), *Who's Who in the Secret Service: History's Most Renowned Agents*

(2018), and *Honest Answers About the Murder of President John F. Kennedy: A New Look at the JFK Assassination* (2021). Palamara appeared on the show in 2014, less than a year after his first book had been released.

Q. How did you come to write your book on the Secret Service and the JFK assassination?

A. When I was only 12 years old, I became fascinated with all things Kennedy and also his tragic assassination. The House Committee also fascinated me when they said there was a probable conspiracy, and even when I saw the Zapruder film on TV, I said, "Boy, it looked like he got shot from the front." Then I saw the film of Jack Ruby shooting Oswald, and I thought, wait, there had to be more than this one man, one shooter. I became fascinated with the Secret Service, which eventually led to my book *Survivor's Guilt*. What I noticed was when I read other people's books on the CIA, FBI, or the Mafia, I noticed the Secret Service pretty much got short tripped. They never really would say too much about the Secret Service. I thought that people need to focus on this, on the actions or inactions of the Secret Service. Most people are looking at Oswald or no Oswald, conspiracy, or no conspiracy.

If the Secret Service had done their typical professional job, President Kennedy would have lived, and we wouldn't be talking about his tragic death all these years later. It would have been akin to the Reagan assassination attempt or the Truman assassination attempt. Kennedy should have lived and could have lived past Dallas. That's not just Monday morning quarterbacking. It is what it is based on prior trips Kennedy took in '61, '62, and '63. Even presidential security during the Eisenhower and a little bit in the FDR, believe it or not, President Kennedy would have lived through it. I'm not looking through rose-colored glasses, and I'm not looking through 2015 security. I'm strictly looking through the security for other Presidents.

Q. What would be the one item or thing that was the catalyst to make you think that you were on to something?

A. On September 27, 1992, the day that will live in infamy for me, I spoke to the head of the White House detail, Gerald Behn. Ironically, this was seven months before he passed away from cancer. He was a very lucid gentleman. He had all of his marbles, and he was only in his early seventies. He towed the official line, believing that Oswald acted alone. He was not going against history as far as the general outlook. I asked him, "Sir, I understand from my reading that President Kennedy ordered you guys off the limousine." And he stopped me dead cold and said, "I don't ever remember Kennedy ordering us off of the limousine. If you look at the newsreels, you'll see the agents on there from time to time."

I was flabbergasted. Behn allowed me to record the conversation, and thank God he did because it's a gift to history; you will just have to take my word for it. I even have a partial video on YouTube of it. It was alarming, and you could hear the shock in my voice. I was waiting for him to say, "Yes, President Kennedy ordered us off of the limousine," because I was going on a different path with the Secret Service. I thought they were culpable for what they could have done. But I didn't get into the realm of them lying about things. This just opened a whole pandora's box. It got me thinking, wait a minute because the official story was that Kennedy ordered them off the limousine. So, obviously, the agents not being by the car, on the car, or near the car opened up President Kennedy to a field of fire whether Oswald was acting alone or part of a conspiracy. And slowly but surely, I started to contact many of his colleagues, because being the devil's advocate, you always think like a defense attorney. That was just one guy, and people might say that he was senile, even though he was in the Secret Service from 1939 to 1967. He was the head of the White House detail during a large part of the JFK era and even into the LBJ era.

Slowly through the years into the millennium, it was like these guys were reading cue cards. I was contacting them all independently of each other, so they didn't know that I had contacted their friends, and they all said the same thing, "President Kennedy never worried about the limousine. He was a very nice man. He never ordered them to do anything." If you read the Warren Report and the official stories, they make it out like President Kennedy didn't want this protection around him. But the 64-million-dollar question is, he had this protection, and they lied about it? Why would they lie? That led me to my book *Survivor's Guilt: The failure of the Secret Service to protect President Kennedy*.

Q. What about the other books out right now, with theories of LBJ being involved in the assassination?

A. Yes, my work is not contradictory to their work or other people's works, for that matter. In my book, you basically walk away thinking the Secret service was really bad and that they should have protected the man. If they had done certain things and not lied, President Kennedy would have lived. Now I'm not necessarily trying to say that the Secret Service was actively involved in getting the President killed. But when you read certain pages about certain agents that lied more than others, you could get to that influence. To this day, I still go back and forth. My first reaction is to say the Secret Service definitely set him up. But was it just gross negligence, or did it cross the line? I name names. All the agents are named, and all the testimony is documented. Even for the majority of people that say Oswald did it, my research still holds up. But I obviously steer towards a conspiracy based on some of the officers with whom I spoke.

Q. So, who were the agents that you were most suspicious of?

A. The three agents I was most suspicious of who crossed the line were Floyd Boring, the number two agent in the White House, Bill Greer, the driver of the limousine, and Emory Roberts, the guy in charge of the follow-up car, the security car that was behind the Kennedy car.

I targeted Emory Roberts because while the shooting happened, he ordered the men not to move. Prior to that, when the motorcade began, he recalled two agents that were running with the car. When he went to Parkland Hospital with JFK, his lifeless body, he usurped his boss's authority and said, "You stay with Kennedy. I'm going to Johnson." He went to Johnson in more ways than one. He became Appointment Secretary to LBJ at the same time he was an active agent. In the history of the Secret Service, he was the only agent to have done that. I can't stress to you how bizarre and suspicious that is. The Secret Service is apolitical; they are not officially Democratic or Republican. They work for the Treasury Department. They are there, by law, to protect the President whether they like him or hate him. They're there for that purpose, but they are not political. So, for Emory Roberts to still be an active agent and at the same time be the Appointment Secretary for Johnson was unheard of. And there's no denial of it. Other agents admit to it happening, and there are contemporary articles that talk about it. The press was scratching their heads and wondering why this agent was fielding questions and greeting the Prime Minister of Japan for LBJ. What's he doing this for? Who benefits? It looked pretty suspicious that an agent who was central to Kennedy's security and let him get killed then becomes really comfy with LBJ. In a press conference, LBJ said, "Emory Roberts couldn't be here tonight. He greets me every morning and says goodbye to me every night." That was the exact same thing he said about Bobby Baker, his right-hand man who went to jail for him for a scandal. So, this was very complimentary.

Q. What about Bill Greer, the limousine driver?

A. If Bill Greer would have hit the gas and obeyed an order coming from right beside him when the first shot or shots rang out, whether you believe it came from the front or the back, let's just ignore that for one moment, things might have been different. Bill Greer knew Kennedy was shot. He turned around and saw him being hit. Instead of hitting the gas, he disobeyed a direct order from Roy Kellerman. So, he had his own instincts. With his own eyes, he saw Kennedy was hit; he saw Governor Connally was hit as well; he hears the scream and the agony and everything. Roy Kellerman said, "Get out of line. We've been hit." Again, he ignored his boss for a second time and stared at Kennedy until the fatal headshot made its mark. Then, all he did was face forward and hit the gas once it was all over. He denied all this to the Warren Commission. He lied under oath, and Roy Kellerman said Bill Greer looked at the back of the car. Maybe he didn't believe me.

Bill Greer had tremendous survivor's guilt and went to Jackie Kennedy, crying and said, "I didn't mean to do it. If only I had seen it in time. If only I had swerved the car or hit the gas." But that night, under questioning by the FBI, he started to change his tune. Playing the victim mantra was born. He started to say, "Well, you know we're always told to keep the cars moving at a pretty fast clip, but sometimes the President told us to slow down." Giving the inference that maybe Kennedy had it coming because he told them to slow down. Play the victim. Kennedy's not around to defend himself.

Q. Other than those three agents that you had questions about, what else did the Secret Service fail to do?

A. The buildings were normally guarded before the assassination, not just during JFK's era, during Eisenhower, Truman, and FDR eras as well. I pulled news articles from the time, from the forties, fifties, and sixties, before Kennedy was shot. And I pulled Secret Service reports and quoted from them.

Michael Torina wrote the Secret Service Manual. If anybody in the world would know, he would. He said, "Whenever the President is in a motorcade, agents or police will guard the building's rooftops."

He wasn't just talking about the inaugurals. He was talking about whenever the President is on parade.

People looked at a still photo of his motorcades, like the one in Nashville, and Kennedy looked like a sitting duck, and they say, "Vince, explain this, Kennedy looks as wide open here as he did in Dallas." The building rooftops were guarded. There's absolutely no question about that. The *National Banner* stated, "As President Kennedy's procession passed, police were guarding the rooftops, and they were relieved at each point." In other words, as the motorcades go by, they were on the rooftops, and as soon as it passed their quadrant, they would be relieved from the rooftops. Also, police were intermingling in the crowd. So, there were armed guards facing the crowds and intermingling in the crowds, the rooftops were covered, and there was a helicopter on the route in Nashville.

This is how they got around the low manpower because, admittedly, they only had about 300 agents throughout the world. There were only about 34 agents on the White House detail. But they were augmented by local police, state police, sheriff's department, military intelligence, and military operatives to help out with the route. So, for people out there that thought that Oswald acted alone, well, imagine if the building rooftops were guarded, they would have seen the open window. And if they didn't see that, the thought that there was a conspiracy would have been ten-fold.

Again, the trip before it in Tampa, Florida, I got the Secret Service reports, and it said during the motorcade downtown, the sheriff's department secured all the roofs of all buildings. I spoke to Russell Gruber, who was a motorcycle policeman in the motorcade, and he said matter-of-factly, "Oh yeah, all the building rooftops are guarded."

Only one-story buildings were not guarded, but that was because they were going at a faster clip, and agents were on the back of limousines. It's not as black and white as people want to make it out to be. When they were going slower, agents walked beside the car or were riding on the back. They had the motorcycle coverage and a good number on both sides to flank Kennedy. You had agents or military or police lining the streets facing the crowd or intermingling with the crowds themselves.

Chief Baughman, the first Director of the Secret Service under Kennedy, was there from November 22, 1948, until he was fired by Kennedy and replaced by James Reilly. He came out with blistering criticism of the Secret Service in December of 1963. He said that it was normally standard protocol for the buildings to be guarded and the windows to be watched. He couldn't understand why this didn't happen. It happened on all out-of-town motorcades.

Q. What about Dallas? I hear that Kennedy was not very popular there?

A. Dallas was a city that Kennedy was warned about. Back in November of '63, he was pro-civil rights. He wanted to end the war in Vietnam. There was a section of the South that hated his guts, and we're supposed to think that there's not one solitary soul in Dallas? But again, that's why I explored all avenues. Because that could have been the ostensible reason why security was stripped, they could say, "We didn't find any threats." But Roy Cullinan, under oath to the Warren Commission under Gerald Ford, admitted that it was very unusual not to find threats in Dallas. I think they did find threats, and they buried them. So, you get a bit of both in my book. You get me going through agent-by-agent, and I come away with gross negligence. But then the book borders on crossing the line into a conspiracy.

Q. Did you check out the agents themselves?

A. I had to make an agent-by-agent comparison and do a mini-biography to explore who each agent was. Several of these agents were on the record, angry at President Kennedy for his private life. It came out in the nineties, with Seymour

Hersh's book. One of his agents, who rode with Kennedy, called Kennedy a "procurer of prostitutes" and some other nasty things. This is a guy that was supposed to guard the President. All he had to do was sit back for a couple of seconds and let it happen. Back then, in the sixty's, adultery was a dirty word, and abortion was a dirty word. Some of them were enraged, and it's on record. So, these guys are supposed to guard him, and they have this kind of ill will against him. I can break it down further.

Nine of the agents on the detail drank the night before in Dallas, including everyone's so-called hero, Clint Hill. He's a false hero; he's no hero at all. When all is said and done, Jackie got in and out of the car on her own. He was the First Lady, not a JFK agent. He was awarded a medal and got all of this hoopla afterward. But in World War II, medals weren't given out for attempts. You either succeeded, or you didn't. This guy drank the night before. Everyone made such a big deal about him, but Clint Hill was one of the nine agents, and it cost the

President his life. Sleep deprivation and alcohol consumption. These guys didn't go to bed until between 3 and 5 a.m., and they had to report for duty at 8 a.m. This is very controversial, and it's rubbed some people the wrong way.

Q. What do you think about the Warren Commission?

A. I think it's a load of crap. Basically, what it boils down to was, America was a very naive country back in '63 and '64. People believed the word of government like it was the word of God. Especially the media, the lapdogs were reporting everything. So, when they were coming out saying that Oswald did it, they believed it. Sure, there were some people who were skeptical, but they kept the skepticism to themselves. And that's how they got away with it. They played on the same thing that I talked about earlier. Everyone's first reaction was that the Secret Service are the good guys. Why would they do anything? That's why the Warren Commission got away with it as well.

Q. I've heard about Kennedy wanting the bubble top removed from his car. Is that true?

A. I talked with Sam Kinney, the driver of the follow-car, three times. He was adamant to me that he was solely responsible for the bubble top removal. He also has corroboration by his own Secret Service report and testimony of the House Select Committee in the late nineties.

Q. What was the biggest difference on the trip before Dallas just a few days before in Florida?

A. This is what happened in Tampa but not in Dallas. Agents rode on the back of the car. A military aid rode in the front seat between the driver and the agent in charge. That military aid was asked for the first time by the Secret Service not to ride in the car. They told him that they wanted to have President Kennedy open for political purposes. Press photographers were usually in a flatbed truck in front of the limo, but that was canceled last minute. Press busses were closer to the car. In Dallas, they were put farther back on the road, and those gentlemen didn't even see the assassination. They just heard the shots. Normally, the number one two agents were on were on the trips, Gerald Bane and Floyd Warren. In Texas, they had a third-stringer. It would be like going to the Super bowl and benching Tom Brady and having a third-stringer play the game. It made no sense. Dallas was a hot town, which meant that it was definitely not Boston. It was hostile territory.

Listen to the full interview on my website at

https://www.alanrwarren.com/hom-podcast-episodes/episode/99af8e82/vince-palamara-survivors-guilt-jfk-assassination-series

The Media

INTERVIEW WITH JOHN BARBOUR

In the last four years since Donald Trump has been in as President, there's been a lot of discussion about "fake news." This kind of talk is not only centered around the current political climate. There have been books written and films released on CIA or FBI infiltration of the media with their agents, intending to change the news that we, the public, hear.

One filmmaker covering this very topic is actor, comedian, and television host John Barbour. Barbour is known as one of the hosts of the NBC reality television series *Real People*, for which he was also a creator and co-producer. He also directed and wrote the 1992 documentary *The JFK*

Assassination: The Jim Garrison Tapes. This film covers the investigation of District Attorney Jim Garrison, who, after the 1963 assassination of John F. Kennedy, decided to investigate further the official report given by the Warren Commission. The documentary hypothesizes connections between the assassination and the FBI, the CIA, the Mafia, the Cuban Missile Crisis, the Vietnam War, and other organizations and foreign affairs issues.

He directed and wrote another documentary, *The American Media and The Second Assassination of President John F. Kennedy,* which was released to specific audiences in 2017 but saw a broader audience in 2019 when it was showcased on iTunes, Vimeo, and Amazon. This follow-up documentary is an extension of his critically acclaimed *The Garrison Tapes* and has received significant praise for its detail and exposition on the subjects of the JFK murder and the evolution of contemporary fake news.[1] John Barbour appeared on the show in the Fall of 2018.

Q. What made you make a movie on Jim Garrison?

A. Well, when I was watching the Republican debates, if you can call them debates, the term "fake news" came up by Donald Trump. I thought, where did I hear that phrase before?

Then I thought that the phrase came from the only interview Jim Garrison ever gave in the ten years following the loss of the Clay Shaw trial. That was on November 5, 1981, when I did it for a show for NBC. But he talked about fake news, and I ignored it because, at the time, I was the writer, producer, and co-host of the show *Real People,* and I had no interest in talking about the media. I went back to the interview and watched it. There was Jim Garrison talking about the birth and use of fake news in the interview I did in 1981. So, I decided that I was going to make a film.

But before I started to make it, I got together with a few producers I knew and asked them what they thought the most important film ever made was. They all said things like *The Godfather* and *Citizen Kane*. But you know what? They're wrong. They are great movies, but they aren't important movies.

Important movies are those that change and improve society. So, the only one that did that was Oliver Stone's *JFK*. First of all, it resulted in the public becoming monstrously aware that maybe the CIA did kill the President, which of course, Jim Garrison proved. Then it resulted in the passing of the Assassination's Record Act in the mid-nineties.

Now you and I know that the military and the CIA are not leaving around blueprints of how they murdered John Kennedy, Martin Luther King, Robert Kennedy, or even Malcolm X. The reason the CIA is fighting attempts to have the JFK files released is that they do not want the Jim Garrison Files released. The Warren Report files are supposed to be released in the year

2039. They won't release Garrison's for another 30 years after that.

When I interviewed Garrison, I asked him if he was called by the House Select Committee, and he said no. He said he tore up the subpoena the way the CIA tore up his subpoenas at the trial of Clay Shaw. By the way, he did not lose the Clay Shaw trial. He lost the conspiracy charge, but he won the perjury charge, the main one he was after, proving Clay Shaw knew Lee Harvey Oswald and David Ferrie. They had 87 witnesses to prove it, and the jury found him guilty. But again, the Federal Government stepped in to stop that investigation.

I will tell you emphatically that this is the most important movie ever made in the United States of America. It's impossible to watch, filled with hundreds and hundreds of facts and proof that not only the Central Intelligence Agency murdered John Kennedy, but in the film, Jim Garrison says, "It was a no-risk operation aided by elements in the media at the spread of fiction before the truth set in." That fiction was spread by Dan Rather and CBS.

When I did that interview with Jim Garrison in 1981, he gave me a list of people alive that should be arrested and questioned about the murder of John Kennedy. Of course, now a lot of them are dead. There are ten people still alive today who should be questioned. This case is still an open case in the Justice Department. The House Select Committee concluded there was a conspiracy to kill both Martin Luther King and John F. Kennedy and handed it over to the Justice Department for further investigation. But they never investigated.

Here's the key and how simple it is to solve this case. Thomas Jefferson said, "You cannot have a functioning democracy unless you have a functioning free press." We do not have a functioning free press. When John Kennedy was murdered, a company or individual could only own five radio, television, or newspapers in America. There was a project named "Project

Mockingbird"[2] by the Central Intelligence Agency in the 1950s, and the purpose was to infiltrate all American media to change the hearts and minds of Americans who wanted peace. To create a society of what George Orwell and Gore Vidal called "Perpetual Fake War."

The first fake war was, as Jim Garrison said on camera, the "Cold War" because the Russians lost 25 million people. Do you think they had any people to fight against the United States?

The enemy to the United States, as Dwight Eisenhower warned us, was peace. Eisenhower warned us of the Military-Industrial Complex and to be aware of the power of it. Well, peace would kill prosperity because the Depression was not ended under Roosevelt until America went to war.

America went to war for five years, and the country was prospering. But what are you going to do when you bring back a million and a half men? How many cars would they make? How many refrigerators would they make? How many will be sold? Everything was modeled after a year. But a bomb goes off in a second and costs $15,000. So, they created this fake war policy.

The next obvious one that everyone is aware of was Vietnam. The most recent was Iraq, with no weapons of mass destruction. The United States is now the evil empire that Reagan accused Russia of being back in the eighties.

Q. So, you are saying all of the news agencies were just reporting the news that the government and the CIA told them to report?

A. We have the head of the CIA admitting that the CIA had 400 assets in every major media in America: the *New York Times*, the *Washington Post*, *Newsweek*, *Time Magazine*, the *Wire Service*, and even the *Readers Digest*. They admitted that these 400 people were writing the news for America.

As Garrison said, Vietnam was no threat to America. The corporations had to get in there to use their natural resources, as we do in every other country in the world. And as Mark Twain said a hundred years ago, if you don't read the newspapers, you are uninformed. But if you do, you are misinformed. That is truer today than it was then because we have no enemies.

Q. What about the Fair Time Doctrine[3] in the media? Has that been affected?

A. When I interviewed Reagan back in 1981, I had to have a Democrat on; then I had to have a Socialist or anybody else who could get 5 percent of the popular vote had to have equal and fair time. You could not have had a Hannity or O'Reilly or a Rush Limbaugh, these conservative empires pumping loudmouths, because then you would have to give equal time to a Gore Vidal or Jane Fonda, or anybody liberal who was opposed to the empire.

The one who got it destroyed accidentally was Jim Garrison. Garrison's major witness was a guy named Perry Raymond Russo. Russo was the one who was at the meeting with Clay Shaw, David Ferrie, and Lee

Oswald talking about triangulation, Dealey Plaza, and the murder of John Kennedy.

The reason he came forward was that after the public arrest of Clay Shaw, he didn't want to be implicated. So, he ran to Garrison, saying, "Hey, I was at the meeting, but I didn't have anything to do with it." And probably because of the fact that he might have been homosexual, because all of those guys were homosexuals, including Lee Harvey Oswald, who was probably bi-sexual.

When Garrison discovered that Clay Shaw was arrested, he ordered his staff never to say anything about his deviancy and unnatural behavior because it had nothing to do with the murder he helped plan.

Anyway, NBC and a fellow named Walter Sheridan, a CIA and FBI asset functioning as a producer, was ordered to go to New Orleans and destroy Jim Garrison's case. So, what he did was get a job for Perry Raymond Russo in Los Angeles for $50,000 a year in an insurance company, and he was going down to confirm this with Russo in a meeting in a motel. Russo called Garrison and told him about the meeting, and Garrison asked Russo to wear a wire. He did wear a wire, and the bribery was recorded. Here was the most major criminal trial in American history, and NBC, the CIA, and the FBI are trying to disrupt this legal trial.

So, Garrison brought suit against him, which the government wouldn't follow up on. NBC should have lost its broadcasting license. The head of NBC, Sarnoff, and anybody who participated in this should have been in prison. Instead, they gave them a half-hour late night of equal time. It really wasn't equal time because the hour they did on him was obviously libel.

Garrison came on camera, and he even did it on *The Tonight Show with Johnny Carson*; he looked into the camera and said, "The Central Intelligence Agency murdered our President. The people who own this country, the one percent that owns this country, your vote means nothing. My vote means nothing. I own shares in General

Motors, and I can vote. And I do vote, but I have nothing to say about the design of the car. Nothing to say about how many miles the carburetor gets. You have nothing to say about how these people run this country."

The owners are looking at Garrison, saying, "We can't have this kind of truth on television anymore." They immediately rescind the Fairness Doctrine and equal time. I am the only critic in America who was challenged by "equal time" that was ruled on by the Supreme Court of the United States.

Do you remember the movie *Soylent Green*? It was an awful movie. What I said about the movie was, "The sets were beautiful. But they would be even more beautiful if they had been placed in front of the actors." This quote was picked up by every magazine in America. The producer of 20th Century Fox sued NBC to get equal time because a lot of writers who had written books that were savagely reviewed got equal time in magazines and newspapers to answer their critics. NBC said no, and he took it to the Supreme Court in California, and they said no, you don't get equal time. Then he took it to the Supreme Court of America, and they said no, you wouldn't get equal time because John Barbour's reviews were of no public importance.

Now on television and in the media, when say MSNBC did a whole hour on Trump with a psychiatrist who said he was insane and should be taken out of office, had this happened 20 or 30 years ago, he could have received equal time and hired his own psychiatrist to answer theirs. You can be maligned on television, in the media, or on the radio now, and you have no recourse except to hire a private attorney and try to sue.

As for the CIA releasing the files, the two most important files were released in the early nineties, and they're both in the movie. The first one was in 1967 from their legal department, saying that they had to assist Clay Shaw in New Orleans. Otherwise, Jim Garrison would arrest Clay

Shaw, their client, for conspiracy. The next most important memo was how the CIA created what they called this conspiracy theory in order to go after Mark Lane, Harold Weisberg, and a lot of wonderful people doing work at their own expense. They tried to align it with UFOs and tin foils.

Listen to the full interview on my website at

> https://www.alanrwarren.com/hom-podcast-episodes/episode/1c30fa3f/john-barbour-garrison-tapes-jfk-assassination-series

---

1. **JOHN BARBOUR** *(Wikipedia. https://en.wikipedia.org/wiki/John_Barbour_)*
2. **PROJECT MOCKINGBIRD** – a wiretapping operation initiated by U.S. President John F. Kennedy to identify the sources of government leaks by eavesdropping on the communications of journalists. In October 2001, the

Miller Center of Public Affairs published transcripts of secretly recorded conversations in the Oval Office during the Summer of 1962. In these conversations, Kennedy took steps, using the CIA, to spy on Hanson Baldwin, the national security reporter for the *New York Times*. Baldwin had angered the President with an article in the July 26, 1962 issue of the *New York Times* that divulged classified information from a recent National Intelligence Estimate. It included a comparison of the United States and the Soviet Union's nuclear arsenals and the Soviet's efforts to protect their intercontinental ballistic missile sites. Knowledge of Project Mockingbird was made public in June 2007 when the CIA declassified a 702-page document widely referred to as the "Family Jewels." The document was compiled in response to a May 1973 directive from Director of Central Intelligence James Schlesinger asking CIA employees to report any past or present activities they thought might be inconsistent with the Agency's charter. According to a memo from Director of Security Howard J. Osborn to the Executive Secretary of the CIA Management. *(https://en.wikipedia.org/wiki/Project_Mockingbird)*

Operation Mockingbird was an alleged large-scale program of the United States' CIA that began in the early years of the Cold War and attempted to manipulate news media for propaganda purposes. It funded student and cultural organizations and magazines as front organizations. According to author Deborah Davis, Operation Mockingbird recruited leading American journalists into a propaganda network and influenced the operations of front groups. CIA support of front groups was exposed when a 1967 *Ramparts Magazine* article reported that the National Student Association received funding from the CIA. In 1975, Church Committee Congressional investigations revealed Agency connections with journalists and civic groups. None of the reports, however, mentions by name Operation Mockingbird coordinating or supporting these activities. *(https://ascensionglossary.com/index.php/Project_Mockingbird)*, and *Encyclopedia of Intelligence and Counterintelligence* (First ed.), Routledge, p.432. ISBN: 0765680688)

A Cold War-era CIA propaganda campaign, "Project MOCKINGBIRD," was begun in the late 1940s under Frank Wisner, Director of the Office of Policy Coordination. Project MOCKINGBIRD sought to manipulate media coverage of the Cold War by recruiting foreign and domestic journalists to serve as clandestine propaganda agents for the United States. It enjoyed mixed success in the late 1950s and 1960s. The program was ended in the 1970s due to mounting widespread opposition. *(https://en.wikipedia.org/wiki/Operation_Mockingbird)*

3. **FAIR TIME DOCTRINE** (Fairness Doctrine) – a policy of the United States Federal Communications Commission (FCC), introduced in 1949, that required the holders of broadcast licenses to both present controversial issues of public importance and to do so in a manner that was – in the FCC's view – honest, equitable, and balanced. The FCC eliminated the policy in 1987 and removed the rule that implemented the policy from the Federal Register in August 2011. The Fairness Doctrine had two basic elements: it required broadcasters to devote some of their airtime to discussing controversial matters of public interest and to air contrasting views regarding those matters. Stations were given wide latitude as to how to provide contrasting views: it could be done through news segments, public affairs shows, or editorials. The doctrine did not require equal time for opposing views but required that contrasting viewpoints be presented. Some consider the demise of this FCC rule to be a contributing factor to the rising level of party polarization in the United States. The equal-time rule specifies that U.S. radio and television

broadcast stations must provide equal opportunity to any opposing political candidates who request it. For example, if a station gives a given amount of time to a candidate in prime time, it must do the same for another candidate who requests it, at the same price if applicable. *(https://en.wikipedia.org/wiki/Fairness_Doctrine)*

The equal-time rule was created because the FCC was concerned that broadcast stations could easily manipulate the outcome of elections by presenting just one point of view and excluding other candidates. There are four exceptions to the equal-time rule: if the airing was within a documentary, bona fide news interview, scheduled newscast, or an 'on-the-spot' news event, the equal-time rule does not apply. Since 1983, political debates not hosted by the media station are considered "news events," and as a result, they are not subject to the rule. Consequently, these debates may include only major-party candidates without having to offer airtime to minor-party or independent candidates. Talk shows and other regular news programming from syndicators, such as *Entertainment Tonight*, are also declared exempt from the FCC rule on a case-by-case basis. Congress temporarily suspended the equal-time rule in 1960 to permit the Kennedy-Nixon debates to take place. *(https://en.wikipedia.org/wiki/Equal-time_rule)*

A Reporter Knew Too Much

SECOND INTERVIEW WITH MARK SHAW

Hearing earlier that the CIA and FBI had infiltrated the media to misinform the public and keep them from knowing the truth, could one reporter have found something about the JFK assassination? Could they have decided to kill this reporter to stop it from leaking into the newspapers and television at the time? We came back to journalist Mark Shaw, who had reported on JFK's father, Joe Kennedy, and his part in the murder of his son. He had now written two more books, *Denial of Justice* and *The Reporter Who Knew Too Much*, only this time his focus was on reporter Dorothy Kilgallen. These were the highlights taken from both interviews in 2018 and 2019.

Q. So, what led you to Dorothy Kilgallen?

A. Well, I'm probably like a lot of your listeners out there, who remember her from *What's My Line*, a CBS show on Sunday Nights for 15 years or so. Twenty million people watched that show. Some people called it an intelligent game show to guess people's occupations, and Dorothy was a featured panelist on that show. Along with Arlene Francis and Bennet Cerf, who co-founded Random House, John Daly was the host. That's how I remembered her.

During the research on lawyer Melvin Belli for a different book, a comment was made to me after Kilgallen was found dead about them killing her, and now they would kill Jack Ruby just stuck with me. I couldn't seem to forget it, so I decided I would research further into it and try to find out what he meant.

Q. So, other than the TV game show *What's My Line*, what should we know about Dorothy?

A. Well, Doctor Sam Sheppard would be one of the biggest cases she's remembered for. At the time of the trial, she was a celebrity. Judges often called her into their chambers to get an autograph before the trial would happen. Doctor Sam Sheppard was convicted of murdering his wife in a sensational type of murder case. During that trial, Dorothy met the judge, and when she walked into his chambers, he asked her what she was doing there. She said that it was the perfect case for her to cover. It had sex. It had violence. He said to her, "Well, Dorothy, the guys guilty as hell." But she said that she was still going to cover the case.

After Sheppard was convicted, she didn't tell anybody about it until the judge died. Later, she ran into the lawyer who was appealing Sheppard's case, F. Lee Bailey. She told him what the judge had said. He appealed the case basically on what the judge had said to Dorothy. That case was overturned by the Supreme Court, and Bailey credited it's overturning to Dorothy

Kilgallen, the power that she had, and her credibility in saying what the judge said.

Q. What was Dorothy's situation? Paint a picture of her life.

A. Dorothy lived on East 68th street in New York City, in Manhattan. It was a few blocks away from the Russian Embassy. She married a Broadway producer named Richard Kolimar, who had some hits on Broadway and played on the radio. They had three children. Unfortunately, Richard hit a downhill stretch. His Broadway plays didn't do so well. He opened some restaurants, but they didn't do so well either. He started to have some alcohol problems. So, he and Dorothy went their separate ways, as her hairdresser would say that she was very lonely. There wasn't any affection there, and he was running around on her. She sought some companionship herself. The first was Johnny Ray, a well-known singer at the time. Known to be a homosexual, but obviously, he was a bi-sexual because he and Kilgallen fell madly in love. That relationship ended in November 1963. In 1965, she was in a relationship with Ron Pataky, a Columbus, Ohio journalist, who was the main suspect in her death. Two to three years after Dorothy died, her husband Richard died as well. It was said to be a stroke, but most people believe he committed suicide.

Q. Did Dorothy know President Kennedy on a personal basis?

A. You hit on a really important note there. Dorothy and JFK were social friends. She knew him at the Stork Club in New York City, and he had come to her home and played Charades and all of that. One time, she took her young son Kerry to the White House. JFK befriended Kerry. He was brought into the library, and JFK gave him a PT-109 pin for his lapel and looked at some letters Kerry had brought in from his third-grade class. So, when JFK died, I don't have the exact quote, but she wrote something in her column, like, "What I remember is a tall man stooping over a young boy, looking at his grade three letters. That's the man who was assassinated in Dallas." She took it personally. That's what really launched her 18-month investigation. She had to find the truth out about what happened to her friend, the President.

Q. She actually went to Jack Ruby's trial, didn't she?

A. Yes, right away, Dorothy was dubious of this Oswald alone theory. The first column she wrote was "Oswald file must not close." She figured out right away that Oswald was a dead end. There was so much conflicting information about him and everything else. She felt that he wasn't the real key to finding out what happened. The real key was Jack Ruby. She ingratiated herself with his defense attorney, Melvin Belli, and there's a picture of her sitting right there with him during a press conference that they had. Then there's a video of Tommy Howard (defense attorney for Ruby), talking about her interview with Jack Ruby, how that happened, what Ruby thought of her, and where the interview took place. It was a serious interview.

We don't know exactly what Ruby told her, but we do know where she headed right after. She not only interviewed Ruby but exposed his Warren Commission testimony before it was supposed to be released.

She didn't go to Washington, D.C., where the government or CIA was. She didn't go to Dallas, where LBJ was. She didn't go to do any of that. She went to New Orleans. That's where she was trying to track down evidence about Carlos Marcello. He was one of the mafiosos who hated the Kennedys most.

Q. So, that must have been quite the feat getting Ruby to do an interview?

A. That was a real feather in her cap. Then, when she exploded on the cover page of her newspaper, "Ruby's testimony before the Warren Commission," you have to think that it was probably like the exposure of Nixon tapes. That's when it became more dangerous for her because there were those who did not want her to expose the truth. And that's what Dorothy was going to do.

Dorothy differed from all of the other reporters because she focused on Ruby. You can imagine that made her an enemy of Hoover, who was shouting that it was a lone gunman named Oswald. He is one of the suspects that I believe could have ended her life.

Q. Why do you think that she chose to go to New Orleans?

A. Well, from whatever she learned from Ruby, she homed in on sources that she had, the best at the time. Then, she homed in on Carlos Marcello. That's why she went to New Orleans. Marcello's back was against the wall. They deported him once, and they were going to deport him again. As November '63 came up, he was in a New Orleans courtroom defending himself against a racketeering charge. Well, he couldn't let that happen. He couldn't let Dorothy go ahead, in my opinion, with writing this book and exposing his involvement in the JFK assassination. So, he was the one with the motive. The one who would say, "I got to get rid of Jack

Kennedy so that Bobby Kennedy is powerless." That's what he did. Then he decided, "I can't let Dorothy Kilgallen expose me as being involved in the JFK assassination. I'm going to have to get rid of her."

Q. Did she have any other enemies that might have been behind her death?

A. Well, I want to go with what's plausible here and not stray too far as many other JFK assassination books have gone. Then, you narrow down the suspects. Yes, she and Frank Sinatra hated each other. She wrote some scathing comments about his girlfriends being floozies. He retorted by calling her a woman without a chin in his nightclub act. We mentioned J. Edgar Hoover. He had the motive to get rid of Kilgallen because if she had exposed her JFK assassination evidence, it would have pointed to a cover-up in terms of his pushing the Oswald alone theory. He could have been in trouble. Marcello was the other one. I also brought into the equation Dorothy's husband because of their marital problems and her not being able to trust him, even though he knew something about the assassination. The fifth one was Ron Pataky, the journalist, who I believe was implicated in her death as well. Those were the logical suspects, and I presented the evidence against them. I presented the forensic evidence that points to Kilgallen being killed.

Q. Let's talk about that last night she was alive and how you think it went.

A. We first heard from Mark Sinclair, who helped get Kilgallen ready for the *What's My Line* program on November 7th. He put fake flowers in a hairpiece for her. She was going to wear this flowing gown, which she was famous for when she was on the show. Sinclair left, and we saw her pop up on *What's My Line*. Sinclair noticed that she was not wearing the snazzy dress anymore. She was wearing kind of a date dress. She was on that program, she was sharp, and she guessed the occupation of a woman who sold dynamite, who will come into play in a little bit. Sinclair speculated, after noticing her change in dress, that she was going to meet with Pataky. She was going to confront him about him possibly leaking some of her JFK assassination evidence to the wrong person.

She went with this producer to a tavern in New York City. Then, she left there and went to the Regency Hotel Bar, which was about six blocks away from where she lived.

Catherine Stone, the 'woman who sold dynamite' contestant on the show, was there in the corner with a mystery-type man. She couldn't tell who he was. They're right together and talking very seriously.

After interviews with Pataky and some incriminating evidence against him, our opinion is that he was the man that was there. What we know is that she was seen there until about 2 a.m. We don't know how she got back to her townhouse, but the next morning at 9, Mark Sinclair, in a very shocking videotaped interview, talked about finding her body in the bedroom where she never slept.

I believe in the book, I've proven that there was no question it was not suicide; it wasn't accidental death either, as the Medical Examiner concluded. But it was murder. And the murder weapon was barbiturates. The autopsy report said there was one barbiturate, but my forensic evidence, primary sources around at that time, said there were three in her system. Based on that, accidental death and suicide go out the window. There's no doubt in my mind that Dorothy was the reporter who knew too much and was murdered.

Q. So, the official cause of death was a drug overdose?

A. Yeah. Let me just ask you this. If you read a conclusion about a person's death, and it said, "A combination of barbiturates and alcohol: circumstances undetermined," wouldn't you want to investigate what the heck they meant by "circumstances undetermined?" But people bought the story and thought this must be what happened, and there was no investigation. Case closed.

Q. I believe one question that came up was why the Medical Examiner from Brooklyn examined her body and wrote the report, even though she died in Manhattan.

A. Yes, it made no sense whatsoever, unless it was directed or part of this whole scheme to silence Kilgallen. Case closed, and nobody's going to ask any questions. Kilgallen's file has disappeared. She has disappeared for 50 years and not even close to being in anybody's JFK assassination books.

Q. Was Dorothy on any kind of prescription drugs, or was she known for having a drinking problem?

A. No, there's no evidence that she had any kind of an alcohol problem. That was her husband's problem. She had a prescription for Seconal, and they found an empty bottle of pills by her bed. But when they talked to the pharmacist, he said that had been about 30 days earlier when she got them. So, apparently, they were almost gone. What they found was evidence of two more barbiturates in her system by some toxicologist at the Medical Examiner's office in Brooklyn two years later. They had been able to save some of her body fluids. They were so scared; they didn't let anybody else know about it.

Listen to the full interview on my website at

> https://www.alanrwarren.com/hom-podcast-episodes/episode/1a47ddd2/denial-of-justice-mark-shaw

> https://www.alanrwarren.com/hom-podcast-episodes/episode/2e5aedc5/mark-shaw-denial-of-justice-dorothy-kilgallen

Oswald's Mistress

INTERVIEW WITH JUDYTH BAKER

Judyth Vary Baker, a woman who claimed to have had a love affair with Lee Harvey Oswald in 1963, was making the rounds in the press as her book, *Me & Lee: How I Came to Know, Love and Lose Lee Harvey Oswald,* was released in late 2011, and people were surely talking about it. Not only was Baker claiming to be Oswald's lover during the time of the Kennedy assassination, but she also claims she was a cancer specialist recruited by the CIA to create a method of spreading cancer to the Cuban leader at the time, Fidel Castro.

Baker had met Lee Harvey Oswald, as he was supposed to be the CIA agent to carry out the attempt on Castro's life by infecting him with cancer.

During this period, Baker also claims she was hiding somewhere in Europe because of the many threats on her life.

Could all of these James Bond type stories have any truth to them? It makes me wonder as she co-authored the book with conspiracy theorist Jim Marrs. James Farrell "Jim" Marrs Jr. had a zest for challenging the accepted accounts of events ranging from the assassination of President John F. Kennedy to alleged UFO sightings and believed that 911 was an inside job.

Even though it was a stretch, I had no problems finding Baker, who was supposed to be in a secret location. I was able to interview her two times. The following are the highlights taken from the first of two interviews in 2014.

Q. So, Judyth, where did this all start for you?

A. Well, for those of you who don't know me, when I was 16, I invented a new method of getting magnesium out of seawater. But because my grandmother had died of cancer, and my aunt was mutilated by it, I was working on conquering cancer on the side. In my laboratory, I was able to give these germ-free mice lung cancer. The American Cancer Society or any of the Universities had not been able to do that. No one had ever done that before. It was in the newspapers and all kinds of articles.

I was invited to work in the personal lab with Dr. George Moore himself. I also worked with James T. Grace, who taught me how to handle deadly viruses. I'm talking about the SV40, the monkey virus that causes multiple cancers in monkeys. This stuff was contaminating the polio vaccine, and all of us got it. They had 98 million doses of it that were sent all over, even to Europe. They were afraid because of the Cutter Incident. The Cutter Incident was one of the things that happened before the second round of sugar cube polio vaccines sent out to the American public.[1]

Dr. Alton Ochsner ran the Ochsner Clinic in New Orleans, and I've become friends with him. He had bought stock in Cutter Labs and had trusted them. He had brought his staff in; he brought in reporters, and he brought in his little grandson, who could barely walk, just a little toddler, and one of his granddaughters.

In front of all of them, to show how safe this was, he inoculated his grandson and his granddaughter. One week later, his grandson was dead, and his granddaughter had polio. The sad part is that California banned it the next day because they found deaths and lots of polio from the Cutter vaccine. Alton Ochsner had lost his grandson and saw that his granddaughter had polio, and he did this in front of everybody. Imagine how he felt.

He realized something else. He realized that we trust our doctors. He had trusted those doctors and researchers to the extent that he had done that publicly. Now he realized they had people who trusted their doctors too. People like Fidel Castro.

Castro, who smoked cigars. Castro, who, if he got lung cancer, nobody would suspect that it was a biological weapon that gave him the lung cancer if it were done correctly.

Everybody needs shots, but how about free vaccines? How do you know what's inside that vaccine? Ninety-eight million people did not know that their polio vaccines contained the SV40.

For the next year and a half, I worked in labs at the University of Florida, trying to make cancer more deadly. Now, why would they want to make cancer more deadly? Remember what I told you about Fidel Castro and his cigars. You had Dr. Ochsner and Dr. Mary Sherman knowing about the contamination in the new vaccine and trying to work out a way to get this vaccine clean so that it could be used safely. But while they were doing that, they injected the vaccine into monkeys to see what would happen.

When they put it in some of the monkeys to see if they got polio, some of the monkeys got some of the most rapid-growing tumors in history. Then, wait a minute, Castro smokes cigars, and we're now seeing lung cancer the fastest we've ever seen growing in monkeys, and guess who was an expert in fast-growing lung cancers? I was. I was trained to handle that stuff. I had been asked to make cancer more deadly. It's in the newspaper articles about me. They were following me around.

I was only 19 when I was asked to come to New Orleans and work with Dr. Mary Sherman. They were getting me involved in a project to weaponize cancer. If you could figure out a way to get it into the recipient, they would get cancer and think they got it from like smoking cigars or smoking cigarettes, you see.

Q. So, why would you help to create cancer that could be given to someone like Castro?

A. Why did I do it? Because I love my country. Because I was told that Fidel Castro was likely to start World War III, and 20 million people could die in a nuclear exchange, just in our country. Castro, just six months earlier, had aimed nuclear weapons at me and my family in Florida.

Now, I personally loved President Kennedy and even sent him a letter to ask how I could serve my country. Believe me, when you do something like that, they pay attention to those kinds of things. So, I was like a super patriot, and everybody knew it. One thing leads to another.

I don't like Kennedy anymore because, by the time of the Bay of Pigs in 1961, he had taken the blame for everything bad that happened there. And I thought he was to blame. All the anti-Castro refugees in Florida and I was dating some of them. One of them was the Finance Minister of Cuba. That was Castro's Finance Minister of Cuba, his son, Tony. Tony and his brother Vincent had to flee to the United States. They went with their mother, who was American because she feared staying in Cuba during the revolution. So, Tony tells me that he knows how Castro had tortured Bay of Pig's survivors.

Q. So, where did you meet Lee Harvey Oswald?

A. I came to New Orleans literally hating Kennedy. Kennedy was to blame for so much and didn't let us conquer Cuba. Well, Lee Oswald would be the one to change my mind on that.

When I arrived in New Orleans, I was 19-years old, and I had been invited to work on a project with the prestigious Mary Sherman. On a project that I know not what it is. That's the key. If only they had told me what I was going to be involved with. But they didn't.

I arrived about two weeks earlier than I was supposed to and stayed at the YWCA. I was in the post office on the 26th of April 1963, and I'm there a little bit miffed because of this man who said that he was going to come and marry me, who said he was going to write me every day. So, I was there to pick up a letter and mail off a letter, and Lee had been standing in the line behind me.

When I went to hand the letter to the man at the counter, the newspaper that I had rolled up and under my arm fell on the floor. Oswald picked up the paper and handed it to me. I said to him, in Russian, "Well done, comrade." He looked at me and answered, "It's not wise to speak Russian in New Orleans." And he said it in Russian.

He had been sent to watch over the project itself. The CIA did not want this project to fall into the hands of the Mafia because they were looking closely. They wanted to kill Castro too. If they could use a weapon like this, too, that would be fine.

Q. You also say that you met Jack Ruby, correct?

A. Jack Ruby, yes. I didn't know his name was Jack Ruby. I thought his name was Sparky Rubenstein. That came about because I wrote a short story about a dog named Sparky. That little dog loved me, but when he had to go to the bathroom, he'd jump on the bed, and if I didn't wake up, he'd pee on the bed. I told that story to Lee

Oswald and David Ferrie. So, when they introduced me to him, they introduced him as Sparky Rubenstein, another dog who couldn't control himself. They never told me his real name was Jack Ruby.

So, when I saw this man run forward and kill my Lee, I shrieked and cried, and I couldn't remember anything for two days afterward. I didn't know that Jack Ruby was the same man. Because I did no research and stayed away from all of that, I couldn't look at any of it. It wasn't until 1999, when I spoke out, that I found out that Jack Ruby and Sparky Rubenstein were the same men. Sparky had known Lee from childhood, from the time Lee was about ten years old. The last thing that he would have wanted to do was kill a little kid that he had known and seen grow up.

Jack Ruby was doing everything he could to delay it. He even stopped to send a telegram. He knew that maybe they would transfer Lee, and he wouldn't have to shoot him. But finally, he went in, and they were waiting for him. Then, they bring Lee out.

We saw Captain Will Fritz was in front of Lee. He moved forward very quickly to one side. Lee was handcuffed to Jim Leavelle, who didn't have a gun out. Nobody had a gun out to protect Lee Oswald. You look, and they were all in plain clothes. All the police were not even within reach of Lee. Jim Leavelle would later say, "I looked over and saw Jack Ruby and saw that he had a gun." Well, they knew Jack Ruby so well, they didn't think he would pull that gun, but he sure did. He ran forward and shot Lee, and I could see in slow motion. I could see the expression on Lee's face when he was being shot on live TV.

Q. What about Oswald's rifle?

A. We know about the two different rifles, the one that's in the Texas Book Depository, the one that was found there, supposedly. But it doesn't have the same kind of sling mount like the one that's in the backyard photos. The backyard photos show a sling mount that was mounted from underneath. Whereas the sling mount that they have on display at the Nation Archives is mounted on the side. They're two different rifles just from the sling mounts. Nobody's going to unscrew a sling mount and drill a new hole in it to put it somewhere else on the same rifle. They are two different guns.

Q. So, Lee Oswald loved President Kennedy?

A. Yes. He said that he wanted to save Kennedy's life. He said he might even fire a warning shot. The first shot actually missed. You know what they called it? They said it sounded like a firecracker. I thought about this long and hard. Lee was on the second floor, and we don't know for how long he was there, and whether he went outside and stood in the doorway, he could have.

But we know he wasn't on the sixth floor. We have Victoria Adams and Sandra Styles, coming down those stairs at the time he would have been coming down. They saw and heard nobody. Lee Oswald couldn't have possibly been on the sixth floor because when they get down to the bottom, here came Officer Baker. Then they spot Lee Oswald on the second floor. He didn't pass these girls. He didn't come up ahead of them or behind.

I now wonder if he threw a firecracker through the second-story window. All kinds of people said they thought it was a firecracker. It's just speculation. I don't know what happened, but I do know one thing, he was not on the sixth floor. I talked to him by telephone only 37 and a half hours before the assassination, and he told me that he believed he had saved the President's life a few weeks earlier.

Q. What do you think of the Oliver Stone JFK movie?

A. Most of it is correct. But he didn't know as much as we know today. Because that movie caused a huge outcry, and it should have. Look, why are they hiding Lee Oswald's files all these years? That was 1967, I mean, it's been 51 years now, and they're still hiding Lee Oswald's tax records. They don't want you to know that he was being paid hazard pay when he was over in the U.S.S.R., and he had to pay income tax on that. He was being paid by the CIA through the marines to get that pay into his pocket.

By the way, after he was dead, Marina Oswald gets an anonymous check for $25,000. Well, that didn't come out of heaven, you know. That came out of somebody's hazard pay; he took care of his family.

Q. So, why are you in hiding?

A. Well, I live in Europe for my safety because of the *History Channel*. This is just one of the reasons. The *History Channel* put on the internet under "JFK Assassination Conspiracy Theories" that I claim to have helped develop AIDS. Do you know how many death threats I got from that? They won't take it away. It's still there. I can't afford to sue them. How dare they? But that's what they do. I got a call once, "You killed my mother!" That kind of thing.

Listen to the full interview on my website at

https://www.alanrwarren.com/hom-podcast-episodes/episode/abe4975e/judyth-vary-baker-me-and-lee-jfk-assassination-series

1. **THE CUTTER INCIDENT** – On April 12, 1955, following the announcement of the success of the polio vaccine trial, Cutter Laboratories became one of several companies that were recommended to be given a license by the United States government to produce Salk's polio vaccine. In anticipation of the demand, the companies had already produced stocks of the vaccine, and these were issued once the licenses were signed. The Cutter incident was one of the worst pharmaceutical disasters in US history and exposed several thousand children to live poliovirus on vaccination. Despite passing required safety tests, some lots of the Cutter vaccine contained live poliovirus in what was supposed to be an inactivated-virus vaccine. The mistake produced 120,000 doses of polio vaccine that contained live poliovirus. Of the children who received the vaccine, 40,000 developed abortive poliomyelitis (a form of the disease that does not involve

the central nervous system), 56 developed paralytic poliomyelitis, and of these, five children died from polio. The exposures led to an epidemic of polio in the families and communities of the affected children, resulting in a further 113 people paralyzed and five deaths. *(https://en.wikipedia.org/wiki/Cutter_incident)*

Jim Garrison

INTERVIEW WITH FRED LITWIN

In reading some of the previous chapters in this book, you have already learned some things about Jim Garrison[1], the District Attorney of New Orleans during the sixties. Some authors we interviewed have a better feeling about him than others, but that's just it, feelings. What about concrete facts regarding Garrison other than the belief that he was a 'true' American or a great patriot.

Fred Litwin is an author who worked primarily with the evidence he found rather than what he thought of Garrison. We had two interviews with Litwin on the show as he wrote two books on the JFK assassination, *On the Trail of Delusion*, and *I*

Was a Teenage JFK Conspiracy Freak, both of which I highly recommend. Litwin is a marketing professional who worked for nine years at Intel Corporation. In 1998-1999, he managed a team of twenty people organizing the launch of the Pentium III in Asia. Before joining Intel, Litwin was Vice President of Sales for LAN Systems in New York City. He appeared on the show in 2019 and 2020.

Q. So, how did you get further into Jim Garrison?

A. Well, the conspiracy theorists online that reviewed my first book didn't particularly like what I had written in two chapters. I had one chapter on Jim Garrison and one on Oliver Stone. One critic mentioned that I had not seen the documents on Garrison released by the Assassination Record Review Board, specifically the Jim Garrison files. The critic was correct. I hadn't gone through all of the Jim Garrison files. So, when I found out they were all online now in the National archives, I decided to start going through them. There were around 200 PDF files, between 102 and 103 pages. And as I started reading Garrison's actual documents and memos, I started finding one crazy memo after another. I started putting them aside until I had about 30 or 40 crazy memos from his investigation. Then I started traveling across the United States, and I went to every archive that had primary Garrison documents until I had looked at thousands of documents.

Q. If I remember correctly, in your first book, you talked about Garrison trying to prosecute an innocent gay man and that the Oliver Stone movie *JFK* was homophobic.

A. Yes, exactly. Unfortunately, Garrison went after this innocent gay man, charging him with conspiracy to kill Kennedy and ruined his life in the process. It was a very, very sad case.

Q. Who was that?

A. Clay Shaw. David Ferrie was another one of his suspects in his case.

Q. Now that you've done the research, what are your thoughts on Jim Garrison?

A. Well, he was in the Louisiana National Guard and was dismissed because of mental problems. They said he was severely incapacitated by these mental problems, and he had to get treatment back in the 1950s. After he became the District Attorney, he became a conspiracy theorist with delusions of grandeur. He went after everybody. He decided to make enemies everywhere, and so he would intimidate everybody, including the police, judges, the Mayor, everybody in New Orleans. Then he went down the JFK assassination rabbit hole and destroyed several people's lives. It's a horrific case study of why you don't want a conspiracy theorist in government.

Q. Do we know who Garrison considered being his enemy?

A. Well, he was enamored with the Kennedy assassination because people were writing books in the summer of 1966. He knew Lee Harvey Oswald lived in New

Orleans for five months before the assassination. So, he thought if there was a conspiracy, then it had incubated in New Orleans. There were a couple of leads about this opinion that Garrison investigated back in 1963 with the FBI. So, he decided to go back and check out these leads. When they went nowhere, Garrison sort of made up a conspiracy. At first, because the suspects were gay, he thought there was a homosexual conspiracy. He started to tell people, "This is a homosexual conspiracy aimed at Kennedy because Kennedy was a virile straight man," etc. It was just ridiculous. I think what happened was that the critics of the Warren Commission came to New Orleans to help him in his investigation. They told him that it was a bit crazy and he had to move away from it. The CIA was a much better target. So, he began to move away from the homosexual angle and toward the CIA.

Q. I guess it would have been easier to say it was the homosexuals since homosexuality was illegal, and therefore they were already criminals and considered to have a mental illness that needed to be treated or fixed?

A. I actually have a memo written to J. Edgar Hoover, by the assistant to the second in command to the Attorney General of Louisiana, saying that Garrison was running a racket targeting homosexuals in New Orleans. The memo stated he was arresting them for money and could Hoover please investigate. They never did, but homosexuals were very easy targets for Garrison. It gave him a variety of people he could force to be informants. So, there was a lot of awful stuff going on, and people in the gay community were quite scared of Garrison.

Q. What was it specifically that made Garrison pick Clay Shaw?

A. There was an overweight attorney named Dean Andrews in New Orleans, and he was in the hospital the week of the assassination. He had double pneumonia and was under sedation. He claimed that he got a phone call that weekend from a Mr. Clay Bertrand asking him to go to Dallas to represent Lee Harvey Oswald. This was before Jack Ruby killed Oswald. So, the question was, who was this guy Clay Bertrand, who called Dean Andrews? The only clue Andrews had was that he said this Clay Bertrand was gay. So, there's an attorney in Garrison's office who said, "Well, who is gay? Who speaks Spanish? This guy Bertrand spoke Spanish, and Clay Shaw also has the first name as Clay Bertrand, and maybe it's Clay Shaw." Now Garrison believed that homosexuals when using a pseudonym, didn't change their first name. So, he became fixated on Clay Shaw, the elusive Clay Bertrand. In fact, Dean Andrews kept telling him that it is not Clay Shaw and that he had the wrong guy. It was definitely not Clay Shaw, but Garrison wouldn't listen.

Q. Now I have to ask you about the chapter you have on UFOs.

A. Garrison would get lots of anonymous letters and phone calls, giving him information. People were coming out of the woodwork to tell him about certain leads. He got two letters at different times that weaved this story about a conspiracy theory on the JFK assassination, and to look into this guy Fred Chrisman. Fred Chrisman was a writer, teacher, and radio host who lived in Oregon. All of a sudden, Garrison became fixated on Fred Chrisman. He eventually subpoenaed him and questioned him, but nothing came out of it because he was teaching high school when Kennedy was shot. In 1947, this Fred Chrisman was working as a harbor man getting logs in Puget Sound, and he concocted a hoax with one of his friends. They declared that they saw flying saucers that excreted some metal. They said their dog was scared, and they created this big story. But what made it tragic was they convinced Kenneth Arnold that it was real, and he contacted the military. The military sent out two investigators, and they quickly realized that it was all nonsense. Sadly, on their flight back to base, their plane crashed, and the two men were killed. All because of this hoax. The FBI was called in to investigate, and Chrisman admitted that it was all a hoax. They decided not to charge him with a crime because the crash was an accident. But Chrisman became one of Garrison's chief suspects. In fact, I bet it was Chrisman that wrote the letter to Garrison, just to get the publicity.

Q. Was there anything new that you found out about Garrison while going through all of those documents?

A. What's interesting is three days after Clay Shaw was arrested on March 1, 1967, there was a communist-controlled newspaper in Rome that ran a six-day series of articles claiming Clay Shaw was on the board of directors of this World Trade Center in Rome, that was really a CIA front to fund right-wing extremists. It turned out that Clay Shaw was on the board of this World Trade Center, and Garrison saw that, so it helped to convince him that the CIA was behind everything. The articles also alleged there was a Montreal lawyer, Louis Bloomfield, who was also the major shareholder of this company. But he wasn't a major shareholder. Instead, he was a lawyer who represented the shareholder. Bloomfield lived in Montreal, died in 1984, and ultimately his papers were donated to the Library-Archives in Canada. They were opened in 2005, and I've been through them. I've read hundreds of letters that he wrote to this manager of the World Trade Center, and there's nothing in there to support the allegations of that communist newspaper.

Q. So, nobody ever tried to reign him in?

A. Not only did nobody try to reign him in, but he discovered the power of the District Attorney. He had the power to subpoena anybody to come to testify before the Grand Jury, which was one of his favorite techniques. When testifying before the Grand Jury, you couldn't bring in a lawyer, you couldn't take the fifth, and when you were finished, he would charge you with perjury, which is a felony offense. Once you were charged with perjury, you would have to get a lawyer. That would cost you money, but it also meant you couldn't leave the parish. You would have to get permission to travel. It would make it hard to get a bank loan or even a job. It was a very, very tough thing for people to deal with. Then, at the last minute, he would drop the charges. So, people were scared of Garrison. You never knew what he would do. He had a lot of power, and he was not afraid to use it. I have a lot of stories in my book on how he intimidated and bribed witnesses and used his power to scare people.

Q. Garrison was charged with bribery, wasn't he?

A. Yes, he was charged with bribery. Back then, pinball games were very popular, and there was a lot of illegal gambling on pinball machines. He was indicted for bribery, and they had his former chief investigator wear a wire. They taped around 375 conversations with Garrison. He took about $147,000 over the years. Back then, that was real money. He was charged, and he fired his lawyers during the trial. He took over his own defense and convinced the jury that he was not guilty.

Q. So, what was Garrison's biggest success?

A. His biggest success was that he eventually wrote a book about his life and the investigation, and Oliver Stone ate it up. So, his big success was having Oliver Stone pay him a quarter of a million dollars to license his book for a movie.

Listen to the full interview on my website at

https://www.alanrwarren.com/hom-podcast-episodes/episode/2e82e452/fred-litwin-teenage-jfk-conspiracy-freak https://www.alanrwarren.com/hom-podcast-episodes/episode/c6595fb0/on-the-trail-of-delusion-fred-litwin

---

1. **JIM GARRISON** (James Carothers Garrison) – the District Attorney of Orleans Parish, Louisiana, from 1962 to 1973. A member of the Democratic Party, he is best known for his investigations into the assassination of President John F. Kennedy. As New Orleans D.A., Garrison began an investigation into the assassination of President John F. Kennedy in late 1966, after receiving several tips from Jack Martin that a man named David Ferrie may have been involved. The end result of Garrison's investigation was the arrest and trial of New Orleans businessman Clay Shaw in 1969. Shaw was unanimously acquitted less than one hour after the case went to the jury. *(https://en.wikipedia.org/wiki/Jim_Garrison)*

References

All interviews were taken from the *House of Mystery Radio Show* between 2010 and 2020. The show airs on several radio stations throughout the United States, including

- KKNW 1150 A.M. in Seattle/Tacoma,
- KCAA 106.5 F.M. in Los Angeles,
- KCAA 102.3 F.M. Riverside,
- KCAA 1050 A.M. Palm Springs,
- KFNX 1100 A.M. Phoenix,
- KFNX 540 A.M. Salt Lake City,
- on my website: https://www.alanrwarren.com/house-of-mystery-radioshow

Below is a list of our guests and their works in reference to the JFK assassination:

1. Holland, Max: *The Kennedy Assassination Tapes*, Knopf, September 8, 2004, ISBN: 978-1400042388.
2. Stone, Roger: *Man Who Killed Kennedy*,

Skyhorse, September 2, 2014, ISBN: 978-1629144894.

3. Barbour, John: *The JFK Assassination: The Jim Garrison Tapes*, documentary, 1992.
4. Mellen, Joan: *Faustian Bargains: Lyndon Johnson and Mac Wallace in the Robber Baron Culture of Texas,* Bloomsbury USA, September 13, 2016, ISBN: 978-1620408063.
5. DeGrilla, Sean R.: *Malcontent: Lee Harvey Oswald's Confession by Conduct*, Neely Street Press, May 23, 2019, ISBN: 978-1733029209.
6. Ganis, Ralph P.: *The Skorzeny Papers: Evidence for the Plot to Kill JFK*, Hot Books, November 24, 2020, ISBN: ISBN: 978-1510755642.
7. Nix Jackson, Gayle: *Orville Nix: The Missing JFK Assassination Film*, Semper Ad Meliora, June 26, 2014, ISBN: 978-0991302017.
8. Fulton, Christopher: *The Inheritance: Poisoned Fruit of JFK's Assassination*, Trine Day, November 22, 2018, ISBN: 978-1634242172.
9. Morley, Jefferson: *CIA & JFK: The Secret*

Assassination Files, The Future of Freedom Foundation, June 16, 2016.

10. Thomas, Ralph: *Silenced! Strange Deaths Of People Who Knew Too Much About The JFK Assassination*, November 23, 2017.
11. McClellan, Barr: *Blood, Money & Power: How L.B.J. Killed J.F.K.*, Hannover House, September 1, 2003, ISBN: 978-0963784629.
12. Caddy, Douglas: *Being There: Eye Witness To History*, Trine Day, July 6, 2018, ISBN: 978-1634241144.
13. Palamara, Vincent: *Survivor's Guilt*, Trine Day, October 22, 2013, ISBN: 978-1937584603
14. Koerner, John: *Why The CIA Killed JFK and Malcolm X: The Secret Drug Trade in Laos*, Chronos Books, November 28, 2014, ISBN: 978-1782797012.
15. Vary Baker, Judyth: *Me & Lee: How I Came to Know, Love and Lose Lee Harvey Oswald*, Trine Day, October 22, 2011, ISBN: 978-1936296378.
16. Nelson, Phillip F.: *LBJ: The Mastermind of the JFK Assassination*, Skyhorse, July 1, 2013, ISBN: 978-1620876107.

17. Litwin, Fred: *On The Trail of Delusion: Jim Garrison: The Great Accuser*, NorthernBlues Books, September 28, 2020, ISBN: 978-0994863041.

About Alan R. Warren

Alan R. Warren has written several bestselling True Crime books and has been one of the hosts and producers of the popular NBC news talk radio show *House of Mystery,* which reviews True Crime, History, Science, Religion, Paranormal mysteries that we live with every day. From a darker, comedic, and logical perspective, he has interviewed guests such as Robert Kennedy Jr., F. Lee Bailey, Aphrodite Jones, Marcia Clark, Nancy Grace, Dan Abrams, and Jesse Ventura. The show is based in Seattle on KKNW 1150 AM and syndicated on the NBC network throughout the United States, including on KCAA 106.5 FM Los

Angeles/Riverside/Palm Springs, as well in Utah, New Mexico, and Arizona.

Read more about Alan on his website:
www.alanrwarren.com

About Vincent Palamara

Vincent Palamara is ***the*** leading Secret Service expert and is an authority on the Kennedy assassination, as well. Vince has written five books to critical acclaim: the best-selling *Survivor's Guilt: The Secret Service & The Failure to Protect President Kennedy* (2013), *JFK: From Parkland to Bethesda - The Ultimate Kennedy Assassination Compendium* (2015), *The Not So Secret Service - Agency Tales from FDR to the Kennedy Assassination to the Reagan Era* (2017), *Who's Who in the Secret Service: History's Most Renowned Agents* (2018), and *Honest Answers About the Murder of President John F. Kennedy: A New Look at the JFK Assassination*. Vince has appeared on *C-SPAN* (including DVD), *The History Channel* for *The Men Who Killed Kennedy*

(VHS/DVD), *Newsmax TV, National Geographic Channel* (DVD), and on documentaries: *A Coup in Camelot* (DVD/ BLU RAY) and *The Man Behind the Suit* (DVD). Vince has also appeared in over 140 other author's books. Vince's research materials are stored in The National Archives and the JFK Library. Vince has also appeared at national conferences, in newspaper articles, magazines, journals, radio, Skype, and all over the internet.

Read more about Vincent Palamara on his website:
www.vincepalamara.com

Also in House of Mystery Radio Show Interviews Series

The *House of Mystery Radio Show* has been on the air for ten years, broadcasting in over a dozen cities in the U.S. It started as a way to interview guests knowledgeable in many of the world's mysteries involving crime, science, religion, history, paranormal, conspiracies, etc. The House of Mystery Interview series is a curated collection of interviews from the show. Each volume focuses on one of the mysteries, providing the background and reproducing the main points discussed in the interviews. There will be no committed answer at the end, as the Interviews series does not attempt to solve the case. Instead, it provides the most compelling aspects of each theory held by different experts. This series is an excellent reference for researchers and a good overview for those unfamiliar with the case. Online links to the actual interviews are included.

Volume 1: JACK THE RIPPER: THE INTERVIEWS

Volume 1 of the Interview Series, "Jack the Ripper," covers the ultimate "who-done-it" mystery of 1888 London. Scotland Yard's "Whitechapel Murder File," in which Jack the Ripper had a starring role, went cold before it could be solved. One hundred thirty-two years later, and the fascination with this cold case mystery continues. Ripperologists passionately debate suspects, opinions, research methods, and theories. Even which murder victims to include in the case is widely debated. Astonishingly, work continues, and today Ripperologists still find new clues that bring us closer to solving the mystery.

The mix of credible and diverse thinkers interviewed includes world-renowned historian Neil Storey, the Godfather of Ripper Research, Paul Begg, Ripperologists: Paul Williams, Tom Wescott, Adam Wood, and Steve Blomer. Michael Hawley contributes his unprecedented scientific approach to the case. Suspect Ripperologists Jeff Mudgett, whose great-great-grandfather was serial killer H.H. Holmes, weighs in, as does Russell Edwards, who believes he solved the mystery through DNA.

Volume 3: ZODIAC KILLER: THE INTERVIEWS

Volume 3 of the Interview Series, "Zodiac Killer," covers another serial killer who has stayed in the spotlight for years after their case has gone cold. It's been over 40 years now, and fascination with the Zodiac is still going strong. Experts passionately debate Zodiac suspects, Zodiac''s letters/ciphers, opinions, and theories. Even which murder victims to include in the case is widely debated.

The diverse mix of authors interviewed includes cryptologist and cipher expert David Oranchak, authors who propose their suspects are already convicted serial killers, authors who claim the Zodiac was their father, authors who offer new or already considered suspects, and an author who argues the Zodiac killer didn't exist at all and that Zodiac was a hoax.

www.ingramcontent.com/pod-product-compliance
Lightning Source LLC
Chambersburg PA
CBHW071429070526
44578CB00001B/45
9781989980224